HEART
OF THE
TRAIL

HEART
OF THE
TRAIL

Stories of Covered Wagon Women

MARY BARMEYER O'BRIEN

TWODOT®

GUILFORD, CONNECTICUT
HELENA, MONTANA

A · TWODOT® · BOOK

An imprint of Globe Pequot
An imprint and registered trademark of Rowman & Littlefield

Distributed by NATIONAL BOOK NETWORK

British Library Cataloguing-in-Publication Information available

Library of Congress Cataloging-in-Publication Data available

ISBN 978-1-4930-2667-8 (paperback)
ISBN 978-1-4930-2668-5 (e-book)

♾™ The paper used in this publication meets the minimum requirements of American National Standard for Information Sciences—Permanence of Paper for Printed Library Materials, ANSI/ NISO Z39.48-1992.

Printed in the United States of America

Contents

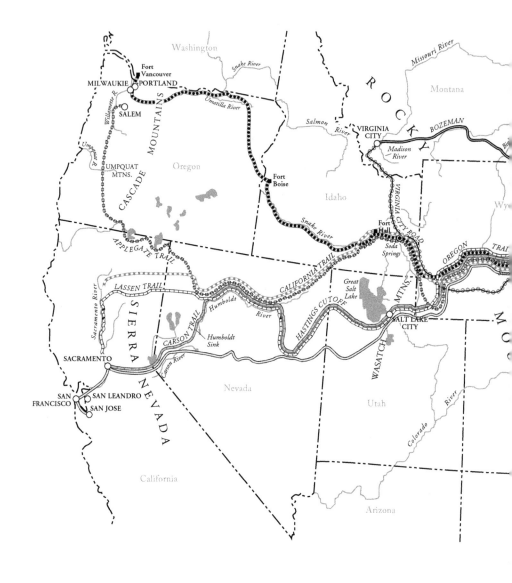

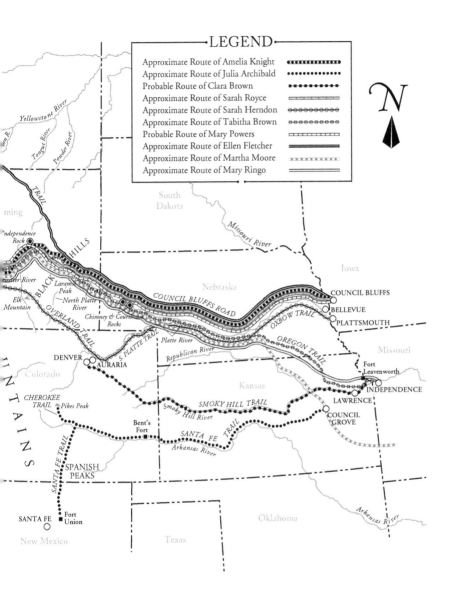

LEGEND

Approximate Route of Amelia Knight	▪▪▪▪▪▪▪▪▪▪
Approximate Route of Julia Archibald	●●●●●●●●●
Probable Route of Clara Brown	▬●▬●▬●▬●
Approximate Route of Sarah Royce	▭▭▭▭▭▭▭
Approximate Route of Sarah Herndon	⊙⊙⊙⊙⊙⊙
Approximate Route of Tabitha Brown	▪▫▪▫▪▫▪▫
Probable Route of Mary Powers	▭▭▭▭▭▭▭
Approximate Route of Ellen Fletcher	▭▭▭▭▭▭▭
Approximate Route of Martha Moore	══════
Approximate Route of Mary Ringo	─────────

N

Introduction

The covered wagons inching west from the Missouri River in the mid-1800s joined one of the most difficult, remarkable migrations in American history. Lured by the promise of a better life, thousands of pioneers left their homes and loved ones to undertake the nearly impossible overland journey into the West.

Some described the first days of the undertaking as a "picnic." Hardy oxen or mules pulled their wagons through miles of green grass and wildflowers, the crisp canvas tops billowing white against an azure sky. The emigrants who strode alongside—with their eyes on the beckoning horizon—were mostly young and healthy.

After a few hundred miles, though, things had changed. The rigors of the trail left families ragged and gaunt. The animals were trail-worn, bony, and slower than ever. Wagon covers had turned brown and tattered from choking clouds of dust. Landscapes were scarred where hundreds of iron-clad wheels had destroyed the vegetation, turning the trails into wide, rutted roads, strewn with cast-off belongings and waste. There were still hundreds of miles to go, and the trails would soon get more difficult.

Braving not only the elements, but illness, accidents, and unthinkable hardship, the pioneers struggled over harsh terrain that included treacherous mountain passes and parched deserts. Sometimes traveling alone, but usually in long, snaking wagon trains, the emigrants pressed westward, mile after grueling mile. Hailstorms and pelting rain stalled their progress, along with muddy trails, lost livestock, and dreaded diseases like cholera, which could cause agonizing death within hours. Tribes of native peoples, disturbed by the seemingly endless influx of intruders onto their lands, attempted to stem the tide. Violence erupted. Disasters were frequent: Wagons rolled over children, men drowned at dangerous river crossings, and snake bites or gunshot wounds were common. Poor water—or lack of it entirely—was a recurrent hindrance. Jouncing over rocks, logs, and into ravines, the travelers worked themselves to the bone conquering the almost impassable trails.

But reaching the West seemed worth the immense struggle.

Women were often unwilling participants in this demanding covered wagon migration, which spanned roughly thirty years, from the early 1840s to the late 1860s. Loath to say goodbye forever to family and friends, most went along only because their husbands, brothers, or fathers decided they must. As their wagons jolted over the two-thousand-mile-long trails, they had to summon every bit of their strength and courage to survive.

Despite their reluctance, women made the long overland trips possible. As they traveled they cared diligently for their relatives and new friends under the most challenging conditions. Often pregnant, they struggled to keep their large families fed, clothed, and safe from countless dangers. They provided meals to renew their party's strength, water to drink even if it had to be toted miles, and care for the sick. They offered camaraderie and moral support for each other, usually sustained by spiritual and religious convictions. When death impacted their group, they comforted the bereaved and took in newly orphaned children.

Perhaps they recognized what an astonishing undertaking their journeys were, because many seized a few minutes each day to write diary entries and letters about the trip. Recording their thoughts was impossible in a lurching wagon, so they wrote before dawn, or after their party had stopped for the night, or for a few stolen minutes while the baby slept. Others penned memoirs after their journeys were over, putting down the travel events they would never forget.

Their writings contrasted with the diaries and memoirs of their male counterparts. Pioneer men, in general, jotted down concerns about covering miles, hunting, finding camps with grass and water for the livestock, or fixing broken wagons. Women focused mainly on the human aspects of the trip. They often wrote about keeping their loved ones safe and healthy. Some expressed overwhelming grief as death claimed those dear to them, and misery as they huddled in cold, wet beds under leaking canvas wagon covers. Others recorded the joy of new births, stunning scenery, friendships, weddings, and campfire dances. Notably absent were references to pregnancy, which, if mentioned at all, were carefully couched in euphemisms. While the men oversaw the necessities of wagons, animals, and routes, the people-centered portion of the trip was largely shouldered by the women, who became the "heart" of the overland trails.

Today, readers can only imagine rolling out piecrust dough on a wooden wagon seat, or tying a churn near the jostling wheels to make butter for supper. More chilling is the thought of bearing a child in the wilderness, or of a fatal illness that could decimate a family overnight. Women went hungry so their little ones could eat. Some gave their last sip of water to a faltering child or worn-out animal. Most endured the emotional tolls of homesickness, grief, and worry.

Many of their extraordinary diaries, letters, and other records still exist. Brittle and yellow with age, a good number are carefully housed in library or museum collections. Among them are the works of most of the resourceful women selected for the following pages.

Amelia Knight gave birth to her eighth child on the Oregon Trail. Mary Ringo lost her husband to a horrifying accident in the wilds of Wyoming, and Sarah Royce faced death from thirst in a merciless desert. Grandma Brown had to abandon her wagon and continue her exhausting trip on horseback. Mary Powers conquered social conventions to overcome her husband's frighteningly erratic behavior. Even the women whose trips were punctuated by constant irritations rather than desperate trouble had their share of hardship. Martha Moore learned patience while accompanying a flock of five thousand blundering sheep to California. Ellen Fletcher, cheerful though she seemed, sorely missed her sisters back home.

The following trail accounts are a small sample of the hundreds recorded. Each writer's work revealed much about her temperament and skills. Spelling and grammar spoke of her background, while wording often shone light on her personality. Fatigue and homesickness shaped diary entries. For these reasons—and for historical accuracy—whenever these narratives are directly quoted in this book, the women's own wording, spelling (or misspelling), punctuation, and syntax have been kept as they were written so long ago.

Individually and collectively, these remarkable women rose above the difficulties of their trips west. With typical grit, they settled into their wilderness homes, striving to rejoice in small pleasures while working to improve their families' lives. For some the years would be cut tragically short. Others would persevere for decades. One thing is certain: The pioneer women whose accounts follow—along with thousands like them—became a driving force that brought homes, schools, and churches to the American West. They earned their exceptional niche in history, and their stories bear repeating.

Near Death in the Desert
The Story of Sarah Eleanor Bayliss Royce

WHEN SARAH ROYCE LEFT HER EASTERN IOWA HOME ON APRIL 30, 1849, to cross the continent in a covered wagon, she had no idea how close she and her small family would come to perishing along the way.

Their trip began with deep prairie marshes slowing their progress, and rain making travel muddy and unpleasant. But Sarah, her husband Josiah, and their two-year-old daughter Mary were in good spirits as they crept over the plains. They were off to California, where gold had been discovered.

To Sarah, sleeping in a wagon seemed strange at first. Raised and educated in New York, she had never camped outdoors. But the wagon was cozy and sensibly packed with the family's bedding, supplies, and most cherished belongings, including Sarah's Bible and her small lap desk. Their three yoke of oxen and one yoke of cows were strong, and their provisions were adequate.

It took a month and four days to cross Iowa. Council Bluffs, on the banks of the Missouri River, was such a popular "jumping off" place for emigrants traveling west on the overland trails that a whole city of covered wagons was camped along the broad river waiting their turn to ferry across. It wasn't until June 8 that the Royces could transport their wagon and animals to the opposite shore. By then the season was late. The family was among the last of the travelers to start out.

They spent a day forming a wagon train with others, selecting a captain, adopting rules, and cooking or washing. Then the company turned out onto the Mormon Trail and, as Sarah later wrote in her memoirs, "launched forth upon a journey in which, we all knew, from that hour there was not the least chance of turning back."

Immediately they encountered hundreds of Plains Indians who were apprehensive about the newcomers. That year, 1849, the native peoples had seen more wagon trains than ever before encroaching on their hunting grounds. Deeply disturbed, they began to take action. When the company stopped they asked the emigrants to pay a fee to cross the prairie. But the wagon train leaders believed the plains belonged to the US government and that they had the right to cross for free. Arming themselves heavily, the travelers refused the request and started up again. They were allowed to pass peacefully.

As they journeyed on, one man in the company became ill, so Sarah and Josiah let him rest in their wagon. Soon he was in misery, stretched out behind the seat where Sarah and little Mary rode. Within hours he died. A doctor from a neighboring wagon train diagnosed cholera, the terrible, infectious disease that pioneers feared most because it was often fatal. Sarah and Mary had been thoroughly exposed, their wagon contaminated. Fellow travelers kindly helped the Royces disinfect their belongings, washing their bedding and spreading their things to dry in the sunshine. As the company pushed on, two others fell ill with cholera.

In her darkest moments Sarah worried that both she and Josiah might die of the disease, leaving their tiny daughter alone among strangers. But Sarah had a strong, unwavering faith in God. She prayed with all her heart that day. Afterward she said that "peace took possession of my soul" and she felt strong again.

The Royce family did stay well, but soon other hardships demanded their attention. They encountered quicksand at a hazardous river crossing and had a difficult time pulling the heavy wagons through it. Next, the cattle were spooked by lightning and thunder. The frantic animals tipped over two wagons, including Sarah and Josiah's, splintering three precious wagon wheels. Back East this would be a minor problem, but out on the plains of Nebraska Territory, there was no wood for repairs. Again their neighbors came to the rescue, donating hardwood boards they used for a table. Once the boards were made into the proper parts, a blacksmith from the wagon train rebuilt the wheels.

On July 9 the party reached Fort Laramie in today's state of Wyoming. Soon afterward, the Royces and another family left the wagon train so they could rest on Sundays and travel in a smaller group. Together they moved on, slowly leaving the plains behind as they climbed into the mountains. They forded rivers, passed famous landmarks like Independence Rock, and crossed the South Pass of the Rockies—a beautiful, gentle route over the Continental Divide.

Autumn was near, so the two families could not afford the time to take the longer, safer trails that bypassed the dangerous desert country west of the Great Salt Lake. Instead they struggled across the dusty plateaus to the south, where the water and grass were poisoned with alkali, and traversed the wild Wasatch Mountains. The Great Salt Lake in today's state of Utah appeared over a rise on August 18, 1849. They gratefully descended into the new settlement of Salt Lake City.

There the Royces replenished their supplies. Time was short as they loaded the wagon with just enough provisions to cross the desert region and the Sierra Nevada to the west. Anything more would make the wagon too heavy for the tired oxen.

An elderly man headed for California asked if he could travel with the family. A few days later, a couple of young men also wanted to join them. Glad for the company, Sarah and Josiah agreed. It wasn't long, though, before the young men's provisions began running out. They asked to share the Royces' carefully measured flour, promising to hunt for meat in return. But hunting in such arid country was often unsuccessful. Food began to dwindle.

For days they inched across the sunbaked land west of the Great Salt Lake. Ahead lay a feared forty-mile-wide desert. Sarah and Josiah had a sketchy instruction sheet for crossing this desolate stretch, but they received more specific directions from a party returning from California along the same route. The leader of the eastbound travelers drew a map in the sand with a stick. The Royces were to push ahead until they reached the "sink"—a place where the water goes underground—in the Humboldt River. Soon after, they were to turn left and follow a rough trail for two or three miles. This led to grassy meadows with plenty of good water. He advised them to camp in the meadows for a few days to let the cattle rest. Meanwhile, they should cut and dry as much hay as the wagon could hold, and fill every container with water. Then they should start out across the Forty-Mile Desert, stopping now and then to eat, drink, and rest. Traveling this way, they could cross the scorching expanse in about twenty-four hours.

With this new information, Sarah, Josiah, Mary, and their companions moved ahead. They didn't know that the guide sheet they had brought from Salt Lake City was incorrect, indicating that the sink of the Humboldt was ten miles beyond its actual location. Traveling by moonlight with these faulty directions, the party missed the turnoff to the grassy meadows before they even began looking for it.

They traveled the whole day across the baking desert sand, expecting at any moment to come upon the road to the meadows. By evening the dreadful reality became clear: They had missed the fork in the road much earlier and were "now miles out on the desert without a mouthful of food for the cattle and only two or three quarts of water in a

Unidentified wagon train travelers of the Mormon Trail
USED BY PERMISSION, UTAH STATE HISTORICAL SOCIETY

little cask." Sarah watched anxiously as the oxen's heads drooped. She knew they could not pull the wagon much farther without hay, water, and rest. She, Josiah, and the others were frightened and thirsty. They decided to stop for the night where they were.

In the morning a crucial decision had to be made. The meadows with their life-giving grass and water must be twelve to fifteen miles behind them. Would it be better to try to finish crossing the desert or go back to find the meadows? Everyone but little Mary, who kept asking for a drink, knew that they would die on the parched sand if they made the wrong choice. They also knew the oxen desperately needed food in order to pull the wagon to safety in either direction. It was then they remembered that their mattresses were stuffed with hay. There wasn't much, but perhaps by offering the oxen a few mouthfuls along the way, it would be enough to keep them from dying.

The desert stretched to the horizon as they despairingly turned around and started back. Each mile seemed to drag on forever. Every footstep was harder than the last. Sarah wrote in her memoirs:

Turn back! What a chill the words sent through one. Turn back, on a journey like that; in which every mile had been gained by most earnest labor. . . . In all that long journey no steps ever seemed so heavy, so hard to take, as those with which I turned my back to the sun that afternoon of October 4th, 1849.

Partway, they saw another small party coming toward them. Their hope was renewed: Perhaps these travelers would have enough feed and water to share. But the other group, although kind and concerned, could not spare their supplies without endangering their own lives. They told the Royces exactly where to find the meadows. To the Royces' dismay, it was at least fourteen or sixteen miles farther.

Sarah, tired and thirsty though she was, began to walk instead of ride in the wagon to lighten the load on the oxen. She vowed to drink very little of the sparse water, giving her portion instead to Mary or to some of the others. At times she lagged far behind the wagon as it lumbered back across the hot, dry sand. Mile after slow mile inched by as the terrible day wore on. When darkness came they stopped again.

The next morning, the oxen ate the last meager mouthful of hay from the mattresses. The water was nearly gone and the day was growing hotter. Again Mary begged for a drink. Sarah knew her little girl could not last long if their water gave out. As the oxen's heads drooped nearly to the ground, Sarah prayed fervently. She made herself walk on, asking God to help them and not to let Mary die.

Suddenly she heard whoops of joy ahead and the jubilant cry, "Grass and water!" They had reached the meadows.

Sarah would never forget her overwhelming gratitude at the sight of the welcome oasis. The travelers rested and refreshed themselves, and then set to work cutting and drying hay, cooking, and collecting water for the desert crossing.

A couple of days later, with the wagon fully loaded, they set out again. The journey was exhausting but, because of their careful preparations, successful. They pushed across the dry sand to the tree-lined Carson River on the other side.

Now only the snowcapped Sierra Nevada blocked their way to California. But it was October; snow storms swirled through the high elevations. Approaching the foothills, Sarah and Josiah were concerned about making it over the steep passes with winter setting in. Still, there was no choice: They had to attempt to cross.

As they neared the foothills, a small cloud of dust appeared in the distance. When it came closer, the family could see two men on horseback, each leading a mule. With their loose clothing flying behind them like wings, they galloped down a steep slope directly toward the Royces. Sarah, well aware of the dangerous mountain crossing ahead, thought the riders looked as though they had been sent from heaven.

She and Josiah were shocked when the men said they were searching for them. The riders turned out to be US government agents sent out to help late emigrants over the formidable mountain passes. They had been told about Sarah and Josiah by the wagon travelers who hadn't been able to share their supplies in the desert. Sarah wished she could thank the worried woman in the group who had insisted the rescue workers try to help them. Instead she said a prayer of deep gratitude.

The skillful government agents helped the family pack their most important belongings, since they had to leave the wagon behind and finish the journey on mules and on foot. They had to hurry. Although the weather had cleared for a short time, more winter storms were coming. In a few days mountain blizzards would make the trail impassable. So it was settled that Sarah and Mary would ride on one of the government mules, and the other animals, including the Royces' oxen, would carry the party's food and most valuable belongings. Sarah selected, among other essentials, her Bible, her tiny lap desk, and a book of John Milton's classical writings. Then they gave a last look at their faithful wagon and said a grateful goodbye to the government agents, who would go on to search for more imperiled travelers. With the agents' specific directions, the Royces started over the mountains.

After two long days of vertical, rocky tails strewn with huge boulders, and cold nights when their water turned to ice, they stood at the summit overlooking California's Sacramento Valley. Sarah looked down into the warm, welcoming land below and knew that she had found her new home. She wrote in her memoirs: "California, land of sunny skies — that was my first look into your smiling face. I loved you from that moment, for you seemed to welcome me with loving look into rest and safety."

The family descended into the mining camps, which were scattered throughout the Sierra Nevada foothills, and set up their tent just days before the mountains were snowed in. They stayed for about two months before moving on to Sacramento, then San Francisco, and finally back to the gold camps.

Over the years, the Royces made their living by farming and selling groceries to the miners in the crude tent cities. Often their home was a sturdy portable canvas house. As time went by, two more daughters and a son were born. Sarah herself gave them their early schooling. The youngest child, Josiah, with a solid education from his mother, grew up to be one of America's foremost philosophers. Later in his life, Josiah asked his mother to write the story of her westward journey and her years in California.

Sarah Eleanor Bayliss Royce is remembered as a refined, educated woman who gave up the cultured things she loved to take a harrowing journey in a covered wagon. She defied death in the desert by summoning her deep inner strength, helping her family reach safety. Later, she braved the rowdy lawlessness of early California, never allowing herself or her children to lose sight of the refinements of civilization. Her story, told in her memoir's beautiful language, has woven its place in the fabric of the nation's history.

Grandmother on Horseback
The Story of Tabitha Moffatt Brown

TABITHA BROWN SCRAMBLED DOWN FROM HER HORSE AND GLANCED anxiously at her companion. Mounted precariously in his saddle, seventy-seven-year-old Captain John Brown, her brother-in-law, was ready to collapse from fatigue and hunger. Tabitha looked at the mountain wilderness surrounding the remote wagon trail over which they had just ridden. Her tired, aching body cried out for food and a soft bed. Darkness was coming, and it was raining. Captain Brown was so sick and worn out that she wondered if he would live through the night. They had no shelter, and only three strips of bacon left.

Tabitha shivered, thinking of ever-present wolves and the cold, wet night without a fire. Quickly she said a prayer for their safety, and for the safety of her loved ones back down the trail with their covered wagons: her daughter Pherne, Pherne's husband Virgil Pringle, and their five children. Their food was gone and their few remaining cattle were so weak they could not move on without rest.

Pherne and Virgil had insisted that Tabitha and the frail Captain Brown ride ahead on horseback. Perhaps the two of them could catch the emigrants in covered wagons who had passed the day before. Tabitha hoped the group ahead had enough provisions to share.

Tabitha Moffatt Brown
PACIFIC UNIVERSITY ARCHIVES, FOREST GROVE, OREGON

Now, in the darkening mountains, she squared her small shoulders and took a deep breath. She had promised herself she wouldn't cry on her trip west to Oregon. So far she hadn't, even when she had to abandon her battered covered wagon and most of her belongings. She wasn't about to start now. Briskly, she took the saddle and saddlebags off her wet horse and found her wagon sheet in preparation for setting up camp.

The thought of spending the night under such circumstances was too much for the elderly man. He moaned and fell from his horse. Tabitha hurriedly threw the wagon sheet over a tree limb so it formed a makeshift tent. She tied up the captain's horse and helped the old gentleman into the tent, covering him with blankets. Then she, too, crouched under the shelter, asking God to watch over them.

Many long hours later, a faint glow in the east told Tabitha their treacherous night was over. She later remembered that welcome morning in a letter to her brother and sister. She wrote:

As soon as light had dawned, I pulled down my tent, saddled the horses; found the Captain so as to stand upon his feet—just at this moment one of the emigrants that I was trying to overtake came to me—he was in search of venison—half a mile ahead were the wagons I was trying to catch up with. We were soon there, and ate plentifully of fresh venison.

Tabitha—a tiny sixty-six-year-old widow and former school-teacher—and two of her three grown children with their families had left Missouri in April of 1846. Tabitha's oldest son, Orus, who with his wife Lavina had eight children, was appointed pilot for a wagon train that traveled six days ahead of Tabitha's. She and Captain Brown, and the Pringles with their children, among others, followed.

It was a "pleasing and prosperous" trip, Tabitha later wrote, all the way from Missouri to Fort Hall in today's southern Idaho. But they still had eight hundred miles to go. It was already August; travel would be almost impossible after the snows began. Beyond Fort Hall a "rascally fellow who came out from the settlement in Oregon" assured

Tabitha's party he had found a shortcut to the Willamette Valley. He persuaded them to follow him, promising he would get them to the valley long before those who took the better-established route—the one that Tabitha's son Orus and his family had taken—down the Columbia River Valley.

Some of the weary travelers, including Tabitha, Captain Brown, Pherne, and Virgil, decided to try the new route, which became known as the Applegate Trail. Too late, they found out the rough shortcut was not yet suited for covered wagons. Worse, it carried them far south of Oregon into Utah Territory and California. Tabitha wrote briefly about the long bleak desert they had to cross, wagons that broke, and weary oxen that gave out. She watched her fellow travelers begin to starve and die.

But it was in Oregon's Umpqua Mountains that the real trouble set in. Tabitha wrote that her family was the first of their group to start into the twelve-mile-long canyon. Of the hundreds of wagons that had tried to make it through, only one had made it without breaking apart. She said the canyon was "strewn with dead cattle, broken wagons, beds, clothing, and everything but provisions of which we were nearly destitute." It was there that Tabitha and Captain Brown were urged to leave the group and ride for safety.

Once they caught up with the emigrants ahead and feasted on venison, the two traveled on. In a few days they arrived at the base of another block of mountains. There, while Tabitha and Captain Brown waited for a road to be cut, the Pringles caught up with them. Tabitha wrote:

Here we were obliged to wait for more emigrants to help cut a road through; here my children and grandchildren came up with us—a joyful meeting. They had been near starving. Mr. Pringle tried to shoot a wolf, but he was too weak and trembling to hold his rifle steady.

As the weather turned cold, the party struggled through the snowy mountains, sometimes advancing only a mile or two each day. After a week their food was gone again. Virgil left the stalled group and set off on horseback for the settlements to procure supplies. No one knew if he would be successful or even if he would return.

Meanwhile, Orus and his large family had reached the Oregon settlements by way of the more-traveled route. Word reached him of the life-threatening hardships being encountered by his relatives on the Applegate Trail. Deeply worried, he loaded four packhorses with provisions and set off to find them.

Somewhere along the route, Orus met Virgil. The two men soon arrived at the starving travelers' camp. Tabitha described that joyful night in her letters:

We had all retired to rest in our tents, hoping to forget our troubles until daylight should remind us of our sad fate. In the gloomy stillness of the night, hoofbeats of horses were heard rushing to our tents—directly a halloo—it was the well-known voice of Orus Brown and Virgil Pringle; who can realize the joy?

Pushing on once again, the tired party finally reached the settlements in Oregon's Willamette Valley. On Christmas Day 1846, Tabitha entered a house for the first time in nine months. It was the home of a Methodist minister in Salem. He asked Tabitha to care for his family and his house through the winter. She traded her housekeeping services for room and board for both herself and Captain Brown.

During the final leg of her journey, Tabitha had noticed a small lump in the finger of her glove. Now that she was settled, she turned her glove inside out to look more closely. A little coin worth about six cents—a picayune—fell into her hand. It was all the money she had to begin her new life in Oregon. With it she purchased three needles.

Then she traded a few of her old clothes for some buckskin and began making and selling gloves.

As the months went by, Tabitha became concerned about the children in the settlements whose parents had died on the overland trails. She realized these young emigrants, and a few children of nearby native tribes, desperately needed a home where they could go to school and grow up. Two missionaries from Vermont, Reverend Harvey and Emeline Clark, and another minister, Reverend George Atkinson, gave their support. In the spring of 1848, they arranged for an old log meeting house to become Tabitha's home, where she could "receive all poor children and be a mother to them." The Clarks and others agreed to help provide furnishings and provisions: "The neighbors had collected together what broken knives and forks, tin pans and dishes they could part with for the Oregon Pioneer to commence housekeeping. A well educated lady from the east, a missionary's wife, was the teacher."

By summer Tabitha had thirty boarders ranging in age from four to twenty-one. The amount of work was staggering, but with her typical energy, Tabitha tackled the job. At one point she planted a garden and served sweet, ripe Oregon strawberries to the children for dessert. The young students fondly called her Grandma Brown. She was in charge of the boarding house and school, which became known as the Tualatin Academy. Trustees, including both Reverend Clark and Reverend Atkinson, were selected to plan for the future.

As the Tualatin Academy grew and prospered, the trustees began thinking about establishing a university. With this in mind, Reverend Clark donated a piece of land. A large new building was constructed on it. The academy's charter was then amended to include a "collegiate department" called Pacific University.

Today, Tabitha's name is inscribed in the Oregon State Capitol's legislative chambers as a prominent early citizen. In 1987 the state legislature named her the "Mother of Oregon." Thanks in part to her generosity and hard work, the modern campus of Pacific University stands amid towering oaks, its faculty members educating students from all over the world.

In the university's Old College Hall, built in 1850, is a small museum that displays some of Tabitha Moffatt Brown's belongings: her wedding ring, a school bell, a black lace cap, a letter written in her beautiful script. Hanging above it all is an unassuming portrait of Grandma Brown, who with her clear, intelligent eyes, still seems to oversee the school and its students.

Outlasting the Oregon Trail
The Story of Amelia Stewart Knight

AMELIA KNIGHT'S HEART POUNDED AS SHE SEARCHED UP AND DOWN the dusty wagon train for her eight-year-old daughter, Lucy Jane.

Of all the hardships Amelia and her large family had encountered along the Oregon Trail, none compared with this. She frantically called out Lucy's name as she scanned the hot, dry countryside just beyond Fort Boise, where the wagons had stopped to rest the oxen. All she could see was scattered sagebrush and boulders.

It was August 8, 1853. That morning, when the travelers broke camp and turned their covered wagons onto the trail, Amelia thought Lucy was riding in her usual place inside the family's second wagon. She wasn't. When the hired driver asked, he was told the child was in the first wagon with her mother. Now they realized they had left Lucy behind. She was all alone in this vast, wild country, somewhere back down the trail.

It had been a long, difficult trip for Amelia Stewart Knight, her husband Joel, and their seven children: Plutarch (age seventeen), Seneca (fifteen), Frances (fourteen), Jefferson (eleven), Lucy (eight), Almira (five), and Chatfield (two). They knew the two-thousand-mile overland trip from their home in Iowa to western Washington was

Amelia Stewart Knight
OREGON HISTORICAL SOCIETY, #59564

not a journey for the weak or timid. The family had heard about the choking dust they would encounter, the drenching rain, and the wild windstorms that could tip over their wagons and scatter their precious belongings. There were long, remote areas without firewood or provisions. Along with the threat of deadly illness came the constant irritation of biting insects—and day after day of the same tedious food.

For Amelia, most of the difficulties could be patiently endured. But leaving Lucy behind was another matter. She could picture her small daughter, terrified and alone beside the Malheur River where they had camped last night.

Suddenly Amelia's breath caught with hope. Lumbering up the trail behind them was another wagon train. Perhaps the newcomers had found Lucy and brought her along. As the wagons got closer, Amelia could see that her daughter was indeed with them. Lifting her long, dusty skirts, she gratefully ran to greet her little girl.

When the Knights left Iowa on April 9, 1853, they were well prepared for the grueling trip ahead. They were healthy and fully stocked with provisions. They also brought along plenty of fresh oxen, including their faithful team, Tip and Tyler. It is believed that the family had three wagons and five hired men to accompany them. Within just a week, though, two of the children had mumps, and Amelia had such a terrible headache that she was sick, too. Pouring rain had drenched their belongings and turned the wagon road into deep mud. Three of the horses escaped and had to be tracked down in the cold wind.

Amelia knew this was just the beginning of the hardships. She recorded nearly every day's events in her diary. In her distinct handwriting she put down the facts—but hardly ever her feelings—about the cross-country journey. She didn't complain, but simply related the daily happenings in a matter-of-fact way that described what it was like to travel the Oregon Trail:

(April 23, 1853) Still in camp, it rained hard all night, and blew a hurrican almost, all the tents were blown down, and some wagons capsized, Evening it has been raining hard all day, every thing is wet and muddy, One of the oxen missing, the boys have been

hunting him all day. Dreary times, wet and muddy, and crowded
in the tent, cold and wet and uncomfortable in the wagon no place
for the poor children . . .

It was an especially rainy spring. The heavy wagon wheels bogged down in soft mudholes. Camping was miserable. Soon after crossing the Missouri River at Council Bluffs and starting across the flat Nebraska plains, Amelia described a wretched windy night when everyone went to sleep "in wet beds, with their wet clothes on, without supper."

During the entire journey, which took more than five months, Amelia's hours were packed with endless chores. Even when she was sick, she had to put in a full day's work, beginning before sunrise. On May 24 she wrote, "weather pleasant, I had the sick headache all night, some better this morning, must do a days work." Her chores included scrubbing and mending the few plain clothes the family had brought along and keeping an ever-watchful eye on her youngest children, especially two-year-old Chatfield. Preparing meals for her family of nine and their five hired hands took much of Amelia's time. She rarely wrote about being tired, though she must have been as she labored her way across the continent. From the beginning she was expecting her eighth child, a fact never mentioned in her diary.

Like many busy frontier women, Amelia found time to appreciate the beauty of the land around her. As the party left Nebraska and entered what is now Wyoming, she jotted in her diary: "There is some splendid scenery here, beautiful vallies, and dark green clad hills, with their ledges of rock, and then far away over them you can see Larimie peak, with her snow capt top . . ."

The weather did its best to discourage the Knights. As the cold, wet, muddy spring ended, the days got hot. Soon the family baked in disagreeable heat. Dust storms whirled across the bone-dry land.

Amelia told of getting breakfast one day in the driving wind and grit, writing in her diary that whoever ate the most breakfast ate the most sand. The wagons in front of the Knights stirred up clouds of dust. During the dry summer weeks, everything, including the travelers and their belongings, was covered with powdery dirt. Earlier wagon trains had trampled and overgrazed the long grasses, forming ruts. Even though the drivers fanned out to avoid following each other, the choking grit was everywhere. One evening in June, Amelia wrote in exasperation, "I have just washed the dust out of my eyes so that I can see to get supper."

Mile by difficult mile, the wagon train toiled westward.

(June 11, 1853) . . . not a drop of water, not a spear of grass to be seen, nothing but barren hills, bare broken rocks, sand and dust . . . we reached platte river about noon, and our cattle were so crazy for water, that some of them plunged headlong into the river with their yokes on.

By mid-June they had gone as far as Independence Rock and the Sweetwater River in present-day Wyoming. Covering just a few miles a day, they climbed over mountain passes where snowbanks were six feet deep, crept across the countryside, and hauled the wagons through steep, hot ravines.

On the Fourth of July, a travel day like any other, Amelia's thermometer read 110 degrees. On top of that, little Chat had a fever, which his mother thought was partly caused by the swarms of mosquitos biting him. Fortunately, Joel Knight was a doctor and was able to help when the children were sick. Normally, Amelia would have covered her son with veils and extra clothing to keep the irritating insects off, but the blistering sun was too hot. All they could do was push on, slowly making their way into southern Idaho.

Even in this dry country, the wagons had to ford streams and broad, deep rivers. At the confluence of the Salmon and Snake Rivers on today's Idaho/Oregon border, Amelia wrote that it was "a frightful place, with the water roarring and tumbling ten or 15 feet below it. . . . here we have to unload all the wagons and pack every thing across by hand, and then we are only on an Island there is a worse place to cross yet."

Although there were long, arid stretches between streams, only a little water could be carried in the wagons because it added so much weight. Sometimes, when the tired travelers did find a spring or creek, the water was not safe to drink because of alkali deposits. Fresh grass for the livestock was just as critical. Amelia wrote that she and Joel fed flour and meal to their horses and cattle when they ran out of feed. Dead stock littered the Oregon Trail. The animals that plodded on had sore feet. Sometimes their necks bled from rubbing on their yokes.

But as the Knights crept over the long wagon road, Amelia managed also to write about the simple pleasures that brought the family joy and comfort. She mentioned that her husband once brought her a bouquet of wildflowers. Another time, they happily discovered tangy wild currants. Amelia made "a nice lot of currant pies" that afternoon. They also savored the fresh fish and potatoes they sometimes bought from the native peoples they encountered along the way.

By late August the party had tackled eastern Oregon and the Blue Mountains, but it would take another long month to reach their destination. Just ahead lay the barren, parched Umatilla Valley. By then the livestock were so worn out that pulling the heavy wagons in the scorching sun would kill them, so the group traveled at night and in the cool early mornings. Wood was scarce, but Amelia was able to make her cooking fires with wild sagebrush.

The Knights encountered the most rugged part of the trail in the densely vegetated Cascade Mountains:

(September 8, 1853) Traveled 14 miles over the worst road that was ever made up and down very steep rough and rocky hills, through mud holes, twisting and winding round stumps, logs, and fallen trees. now we are on the end of a log, now bounce down in a mud hole, now over a big root of a tree, or rock, then bang goes the other side of the wagon and woe to be whatever is inside.

(September 9, 1853) . . . there is no end to the wagons, buggys ox yokes, chains, ect [sic] that are lying all along this road some splendid good wagons just left standing.

Other travelers had to abandon their covered wagons, but the Knight family was able to get theirs through to the end of the trip. Amelia did tell of leaving her pickles and a few other belongings behind on the trail, since they were too "unhandy" to carry. At one point they split up the wagon's deck boards to make firewood and lighten the load. Here again, Amelia threw out "a good many things."

By mid-September the family could see the journey's end. Near Milwaukie, Oregon, just across the Columbia River from their destination, the drizzling rain began again. Amelia wrote with great weariness: (September 13) "We may now call ourselves through, they say. Here we are in Oregon making our camp in an ugly bottom, with no home, except our wagons and tent, it is drizzling and the weather looks dark and gloomy."

After four more rainy days, Amelia's diary ends. Her eighth child was born the next day. She named him Wilson Carl Knight after the hired driver of their second wagon.

Soon after Amanda gave birth, the tired family ferried across the Columbia River to the new Territory of Washington, a process said to have taken three days. There, about ten miles upstream from

Vancouver, Washington, they are believed to have traded two yokes of oxen for a piece of land and a small log cabin. This is where they made their new home, which would become the family farm for many years.

Amelia was well educated for the time; she also taught and encouraged her children to study. They grew up to become prominent citizens. Her husband Joel was active in community affairs. He often represented Clark County at the Territorial Legislature. In 1867, fourteen years after the family settled in Washington, Joel died of tuberculosis. Amelia remarried, but her second marriage did not last. She was elderly when she died in 1896 and was buried beside Joel in the Knight Cemetery on the north bank of the Columbia River.

Amelia Stewart Knight showed exceptional strength on her westward journey. Exhausted but resolute, she undoubtedly wrote parts of her journal while wearily sitting beside her battered wagon in smoky firelight. With her youngest children asleep, she could take a few minutes to sink onto the ground, her pen in her calloused hand, to record the day's events. Other times, she must have written while cramped in the damp, dark family tent, or sitting in the stifling heat of the sunbaked wagon. Her well-chosen words probably seemed ordinary to her then. Little did she know that generations later, readers would be inspired by her patience and hard work—and by the way she made certain her family outlasted the Oregon Trail.

Chilling Journey
The Story of Mary Rockwood Powers

MARY POWERS WATCHED HER HUSBAND, DR. AMERICUS POWERS, lead their tired horses through a hip-deep stream. Who was this man she had married? The westward journey had turned him into someone she hardly knew. He had once been a considerate husband, but was now sullen and unpredictable. How would she and her three young children ever reach California if he kept behaving so strangely? And what about their poor horses, so worn out they wobbled in the harness as they pulled the heavy covered wagon?

Fort Laramie was just ahead. After days of travel on the Old Mormon Trail that spring of 1856, Mary was eager to reach the fort because her husband had promised to trade the weak horses for some sturdy oxen there. She hoped they could make it that far. To help the time go more quickly, Mary quietly prayed and read *Pilgrim's Progress* to the children—Sarah, Cephas, and Celia. She wrote a long letter to her mother and sisters back home and kept a diary.

Mary's devotion to her children was clear. She loved them deeply and cared for them with all her energy. When a cold hailstorm thundered down one dark, windy night on the unsheltered plains, she protected them by crouching in the wagon and holding a blanket over the

Mary Rockwood Powers and Dr. Americus W. Powers
REPRINTED FROM *SOME ANNALS OF THE POWERS FAMILY*

front opening. After the two-hour storm was over, Mary was soaked with icy water and so stiff her husband had to help her move. The children still slept, safely nestled in their blankets.

Already it seemed as if they had been on the road forever. An acquaintance had borrowed their precious rifle and never returned it, leaving the family with no way to hunt or protect themselves. Mary had lost track of the days. Worse than that, the wagon train they had joined left them behind "to get along the best we could." Mary wrote that it was because the exhausted horses couldn't keep up, but it was highly unusual for a company to abandon one of its families. Historians speculate that perhaps Dr. Powers's erratic, moody behavior caused the split.

From Mary's descriptive writings, it's plain that the journey had been hard on him. At one point on the trip, she wrote that he had "grown so peculiar" and that "For some days the Doctor had been falling into his old sullen mood again; out of humor with everyone, and the more kindness anyone showed us the worse he got." Dr. Powers avoided others, sometimes not speaking to them unless it was to argue, and he refused to ask for help even when his family was in danger.

It was obvious that the doctor's decision to buy beautiful, expensive horses to make the trip across the overland trail had been a mistake. The wagon weighed nine hundred pounds empty; filled with household goods and provisions, it was far too heavy for fine horses, even on flat, dry stretches. Steep, rocky, or muddy parts of trail wore the animals to the bone. Mary bit her tongue. She tried her best to make the journey successful by caring for her children, preparing the meals, and taking care of the domestic chores.

But when Dr. Powers passed Fort Laramie and then the next fort without trading for oxen or buying flour, Mary was paralyzed with fear. Had her husband lost his mind? The family was nearly out of food, having fed some of their flour to the horses. She was terrified to enter what the emigrants sometimes called the Black Hills (known today as the Laramie Mountains) without supplies or reliable oxen. Again and again, the doctor promised to take care of the problems, but each time he failed to act. Day after day he hitched the half-dead horses to the wagon.

His odd ways frightened and baffled Mary, but true to the customs of the time, she held back her comments. It was only in letters to her mother and sisters that she recalled her worst days on the journey, saying she feared she was traveling with "a maniac." "I felt as though myself and little ones were at the mercy of a mad man. It did not seem that any man in his right mind would take the course the Doctor was taking. I said nothing but thought the more."

On and on the family struggled. Dr. Powers had to alternate their spent horses every few hundred yards to let them rest. The animals foamed at the mouth. They were so stiff and worn out they could hardly stand; one leaned against another for support. Sometimes they collapsed in the harness. Mary ached for them. She would gladly have walked all the way to California to save them her weight in the wagon, but she was expected to drive the team.

Up and down hills, through ravines, and across streams they traveled, bumping over rocks and going, as Mary put it, "inch by inch at a time." Finally, it became evident that she had to take matters into her own hands. She told her husband that if he failed to trade for oxen at the next opportunity, then she would. They had come upon an emigrant party, and the doctor again promised he would make arrangements in the morning.

The next day Dr. Powers did ask to trade, but he waited until it was too late. The emigrants needed to get on the road, so they were reluctant to take the time. Gathering her courage, Mary spoke to the leader, Mr. Hendrick, herself. He assured her that if the family could travel with their own horses one more day, the company would lend them some oxen that evening. That day, one of the horses nearly died. The other animals slowly dragged the clumsy wagon over the hills, but finally made it to camp. True to his word, Mr. Hendrick appeared with three teams of oxen Mary could borrow. Several families offered them dried apples, beans, and fresh game or fish. Gratefully, she accepted. By then she and the doctor had only three dollars left.

To Mary's horror it wasn't long before Dr. Powers had a disagreement with the others in the train. Harsh words were exchanged, and the doctor broke away from the party. (Gentle, refined Mary wrote in her diary, "I forbear giving the details.") The wagon train women kindly shared gifts with Mary, who already had become their friend, and said goodbye with "tears running down their sunburnt cheeks." Mary reported that the men were so concerned for her that they, too, shed tears. After returning the borrowed oxen, the little family went on alone.

Fortunately, they were only several days from the settlements at Salt Lake, but by then two of the horses had died and the others were back in the harness again. Laboring on step by step, so worn they could "hardly crawl," Mary wrote, the animals brought the wagon to a creek with steep banks. They got the wagon down into the creek bed but could not pull it up the other side. Dr. Powers and Mary unloaded the children and their belongings, and unhitched the horses. They led the animals to the top of the bank where the footing was better and tied them to the wagon with a long rope. Mary was instructed to hold up the wagon tongue and then quickly jump aside as the horses pulled the wagon up the incline.

Something went wrong. The heavy wagon started up the steep bank, but before Mary could spring out of the way, it slipped back down. Its huge iron-rimmed wheels ran over her ankle. Thanks to the soft gravel underfoot, Mary's ankle was badly bruised but not broken.

Finally, they arrived at the Mormon settlements near Salt Lake, where they rested for several days and tended their horses. The Mormon settlers invited the Powers family to stay with them, gave them food and desperately needed supplies, and allowed them to graze the horses. Mary returned their generosity as best she could, sharing thread, stockings, and coffee. She traded two white blankets for two hundred pounds of flour. By mid-August the horses were ready to move on.

It was then an incident occurred that had devastating effects on Mary. One afternoon, the family reached a steep incline. The horses could not pull the wagon up without stopping to rest every few feet. Mary was to block the wheels with boulders when they halted so the wagon would not roll back down. She spent the afternoon lugging the big rocks up the slope, blocking the wheels, and lugging them some more. The two youngest children needed help up, too, and Mary carried them to the top. When the wagon reached level ground at last, she was trembling and sick from exhaustion. From that day on, her health was never the same. For the rest of the trip, she could not walk more than a few yards without being overcome by weakness and shakiness, and she was almost always tired.

Beyond Salt Lake the Powers family met a sheep train—a small company driving a flock of sheep west. Traveling with them for a few days, Mary befriended them, although her husband remained distant and angry. Mr. Curtis, who owned part of the flock, couldn't help noticing Dr. Powers's peculiar behavior. He quietly assured Mary that he and the others would care for her and the children. This was the most dangerous part of the route, he told her, and she needn't fear being abandoned. He talked Dr. Powers into borrowing some of the sheep train's horses, and shared their precious dried beef and cheese. Mary gratefully repaid their kindness with a bar of soap, and used the last of her dried strawberries and nutmeg to make them a shortcake.

Soon the party met a wagon train going to California, where the Powers family was headed. Mr. Curtis helped Dr. Powers contract to travel with the company, who agreed to escort them across the desert country ahead. A capable traveler named Major Whitesides abandoned his wagon and put his belongings into theirs so they could use his oxen. He drove, relieving a weak and tired Mary of the responsibility.

The wagon train crossed the vast, dangerous deserts of today's Nevada. Mary watched another horse die in agony, despite her feeding him precious flour, and she made coffee out of such foul-tasting water that she never liked coffee again. Ever thoughtful of her children, she tucked away a large bottle of clean water for them and rationed it out sparingly when all the other water was gone. At night she lay awake in the wagon while the others slept. Worry and fear clouded her mind. She was cramped between her husband and children since they had long ago stopped setting up their sleeping tent. Always weary, she sometimes took afternoon naps in the hot, lurching wagon.

By the time they reached the Sierra Nevada, Dr. Powers's contract with the wagon train had expired, and the family was traveling alone again. They had been offered a donkey that was hitched with their last remaining horse, Blackey. Struggling over the mountains, Mary continued to care for her children, even though her health was poor. Once again their flour was gone.

Finally, on October 8, 1856, they inched into the Sacramento Valley. Mary remembered feeling desperate to get out of the wagon, but when she tried to walk, she trembled so badly she could hardly stand. Using a stick for a cane, she struggled down the last hill, hearing her husband's shouts to hurry up, but not being able to go any faster. When she reached the others, she was so weak she had to be lifted into the wagon.

California was rich with freshly harvested foods. The half-starved family delighted in the tomatoes, cabbage, beets, and watermelon that other settlers shared with them. As Mary tried to regain her strength, she thanked God for sparing her three treasured children on the long, hard journey.

The five of them took a boat down the river to a tiny cabin near San Leandro, California. This would be their home. Mary said that despite its miserable floor, it had a good roof and she made it "quite comfortable." Dr. Powers planted potatoes, which thrived in the dark soil. Mary wrote about how hard he worked to provide for his family and how devoted he had become since they settled down.

Mary rejoiced when she found letters from home at the post office. She was thrilled to receive a trunk that had been sent by ship, filled with desperately needed clothing and other supplies. Everywhere she went, she made new friends. She tried to improve her health, but the grueling overland trip had taken a terrible toll on her, and day-to-day frontier life was demanding. As she struggled to cope, she realized she was pregnant.

The following June, twins were born. The babies were beautiful and alert, and Mary adored them. Despite her fatigue, she rocked and held them day and night. But within six months, both infants had died, probably of illness. She grieved with all her heart.

Mary seemed to know her own life was near its end. She wrote home: ". . . but dear mother I much fear we shall never meet again except in the spirit land." Two months later, on May 1, 1858, Mary died.

Even on the verge of death, Mary continued to care for her three children. Her last wish was that they be sent East to be brought up and educated by her mother. Mary never knew that two of them would die in childhood and the third, Sarah, would grow up in the wilds of California with little opportunity for education or culture. Sarah taught herself to write by copying her grandmother's letters.

Mary Rockwood Powers endured—with courage and restraint— a chilling journey that today can hardly be imagined. Despite the anguish of the trip, she devoted herself to her loved ones and learned to take charge when her husband's unstable behavior endangered the family's welfare. Her long-ago letters and diary offer a clear picture of this remarkable woman who sacrificed her health bringing her family safely across the overland trail.

To the Summit in Bloomers
The Story of Julia Anna Archibald

TWENTY-YEAR-OLD JULIA ANNA ARCHIBALD* PUT THE FINISHING touches on her writing for the day. The sun was rising, spreading its rosy light over the Kansas prairie. It glowed through the wagon's canvas cover, inviting her to linger in its warmth. She knew, though, that it was time to step outside and make the breakfast campfire; soon the party would hitch up and start another day of travel.

Tucking her precious pen in a safe place, she reread what she had written before wrapping the pages in a clean flour sack to keep the dust off. In the accounts she was sending to her mother and a small feminist newspaper in the East, Julia described the 1858 journey she was taking from Lawrence, Kansas, to the gold fields at Pikes Peak. Her poetic words told of her summer's trip on the Santa Fe Trail.

She traveled with her new husband, a bold and daring man named James Henry Holmes, and her eighteen-year-old brother, Albert W. Archibald. Young, hopeful, and adventurous in spirit, the three hoped to find gold at the end of their trip, but were even more eager to see the spectacular Rocky Mountains.

* In keeping with her belief in equal rights, Julia frequently used her maiden name instead of the surname of her husband.

Julia Anna Archibald (Holmes)
THE DENVER PUBLIC LIBRARY, WESTERN HISTORY COLLECTION, F-7348

Julia was an intelligent woman who believed that men and women should be treated equally. Her attitudes and writings had been influenced by her parents. Her mother was a women's rights supporter and a personal friend of the famous suffrage crusader Susan B. Anthony. Her father was an antislavery activist.

Julia, or "Annie," as she was sometimes called, was proud of her bold decision not to wear traditional long dresses on the trail. Instead, she wore bloomers—a short skirt over a pair of baggy pants. Even though bloomers were considered somewhat scandalous, Julia felt the full, toe-length dresses of the day would get in her way on the outdoor journey. She enjoyed wandering through the deep, waving grasses in search of wildflowers, which her comfortable attire gave her the freedom to do.

As the wagons set out on their journey, she wrote:

Nearly all the men were entire strangers to me, and as I was cooking our dinner some of them crowded around our wagon, gazing sometimes at the stove . . . but oftener on my dress, which did not surprise me, for, I presume, some of them had never seen just such a costume before.

Julia felt so strongly about wearing bloomers that she had trouble forming a friendship with the only other woman on the wagon train, Mrs. Middleton, who wore long skirts. Mrs. Middleton begged Julia to wear traditional clothing because the men of the party talked among themselves about how odd the bloomers looked. Julia replied that she could not dress to please others.

She also asked the wagon train's guardmaster if she could take her turn at guarding the camp, a job customarily only for men:

I signified to the Guardmaster that I desired to take my turn with the others in the duty of guarding the camp, and requested to have

*my watch assigned with my husband. The captain of the guard . . .
was of the opinion that it would be a disgrace to the gentlemen of
the company for them to permit a woman to stand on guard.*

Julia, although disturbed at the guardmaster's refusal, turned her attention to other things. She studied wildflowers, wrote in her journal, taught her brother the Lord's Prayer in Spanish, and improved her physical fitness by walking longer and longer distances each day.

As the wagons pressed on, Julia wrote about the presence of Cheyenne and Arapaho tribesmen, describing them in her letters as "large, finely formed, and noble looking men" who visited the wagon train bringing messages or wanting to trade.

For about three hundred miles, the wagons roughly followed the Arkansas River. Julia commented that although the river was scenic, "the current is so swift that it is very unpleasant bathing—that delightful and grateful recreation to the dusty traveler." By late June the travelers had reached Bent's Fort, a large adobe fortress with four-foot-thick walls located on a bluff overlooking the upper Arkansas River in what is now Colorado. A few days later, on the Fourth of July and just a month after the wagons started out, a snowy mountain appeared in the distance. Rising high into the sky, it stood out from the rest of the majestic Rockies. It was Pikes Peak, their destination. They felt sure they would find gold among its foothills.

Four days later, they camped as close to the mountains as they could get in the heavy wagons. They would remain there for more than a month while the prospectors among them made excursions to look for the precious metal. Oddly enough, Julia's letters didn't mention whether she, James, and her brother spent time searching for gold, or if they found any.

To her knowledge, no woman and very few men had ever made the hazardous, difficult climb to the snowy summit of the beautiful mountain. She and her husband decided to try. Julia was in strong physical condition from her long walks. Late in July, tiring of the monotony of camp life, she filled her backpack with hiking supplies, including food, a quilt, and some clothing. James carried food, camping gear, some writing materials, and a treasured book of Ralph Waldo Emerson's essays. They planned to be gone for six days.

In her journal Julia recorded the highlights of the climb, beginning on August 1, 1858. At first they hiked through the undisturbed foothills, crossing at least one knee-deep stream so cold it made her feet ache. Then they reached the mountain itself. Julia thrilled at the fragrant evergreens, the crystal clear mountain creeks tumbling down the ravines, and the variety of "bewitchingly beautiful" wildflowers.

By August 4 Julia and James had climbed to within two steep miles of the summit. They made a base camp on the mountainside where they could see distant covered wagons and tents on the hazy plains below. There, in a mossy sheltered place they named Snowdell, they spent a day writing, resting, and admiring the landscape. The next day, August 5, they set off for the rocky peak, carrying only their writing materials and their Emerson book. Near the top, the climb became much harder as they came upon enormous piles of stones that were difficult to scale.

When the couple finally reached the cold, windy summit of Pikes Peak at an altitude of more than fourteen thousand feet, Julia rejoiced in their accomplishment. She thought she was possibly the first woman ever to stand at the top. Shivering but exultant, they left their names on a large boulder and stayed to write some letters. Julia put down these words to her mother:

I have accomplished the task which I marked out for myself, and now I feel amply repaid for all my toil and fatigue. Nearly every one tried to discourage me from attempting it, but I believed that I

should succeed; and now here I am, and feel that I would not have
missed this glorious sight for anything at all.

Before leaving the summit, Julia read aloud some beloved words
from Emerson. Then, as a summer snowstorm swirled around them,
Julia and James hurried partway down the vast mountain. The next day,
tired but satisfied, they arrived back at the wagon train.

The prospectors in the party apparently did discover a small
amount of gold at Pikes Peak, which perhaps drew others to the area.
Later on, several larger gold strikes were made nearby. But most of the
group, including Julia, her husband, and her brother, wanted to push
on to New Mexico in search of bigger deposits. Nearly all of them
turned their wagons toward the warm Spanish Peaks area to continue
hunting gold during the winter.

Julia and her husband spent the next few years in New Mexico,
where James was appointed secretary of the territory by President
Abraham Lincoln. Julia was a correspondent for the *New York Herald*
Tribune. They eventually had four children: two sons and two daughters. During the last years of the Civil War, the family moved to Washington, DC, where Julia and James divorced. There Julia lived out her
life working in federal agencies and continuing her efforts on behalf of
women's organizations.

Today we remember Julia standing strong, determined, and proud
at the summit of Pikes Peak, her bloomer costume flapping in the icy
wind. Looking east, she could see the brown plains she had crossed to
reach her destination. Looking west, she saw new frontiers that offered
hope for the ideals of feminism she held dear. With her independent
thinking and the words she wrote on her pioneer journey, Julia Anna
Archibald helped bring the issue of women's rights to the American
West.

"I Lift My Lamp"*
The Story of Clara Brown

CLARA BROWN TURNED THE SAVORY BISON ROAST IN THE HEAVY Dutch oven and heaped on more campfire coals. She needed to stew some dried apples and bake more biscuits, too—enough to provide dinner and breakfast for a passel of hungry men. The wagon drivers for whom she was hired to cook could gobble up a whole buttery biscuit in a single mouthful! She'd be working late tonight and up again tomorrow long before dawn.

All day, Clara had trudged beside the covered wagons. The ground under her aching feet was dusty that hot day in 1859. The sun beat down on her skin. But she held her graying head high and her back straight as she walked, one step after another, to her new home in the West.

Clara was a recently freed slave in her late fifties. Historical accounts differ about whether Clara was set free or whether she finally saved enough money to buy her own freedom, but afterward she had moved to Leavenworth, Kansas Territory. There she'd worked as a household cook and a laundress.

* "I lift my lamp beside the golden door!"—from the inscription on the Statue of Liberty (Emma Lazarus).

Years before her emancipation, Clara had endured the most terrible of heartbreaks: Her husband, her son, and her two living daughters had been sold away from her. She was left with a permanent empty place in her heart. Only her steadfast faith in God sustained her. From what she could learn now, it seemed that just one of her beloved family was still alive—her grown daughter Eliza Jane. Clara's fondest dream was to find her someday.

Clara wondered if Eliza Jane might be in western Kansas Territory (today's state of Colorado), where people were flocking by the thousands seeking gold. When she heard about a freight company of covered wagons hauling goods from Leavenworth to Pikes Peak, she asked to go along as far as Denver. The freighters agreed, if she would cook for some of the company's men on the eight-week journey. Researchers believe that she, like the others, would walk the seven hundred miles, since the wagons would have been packed to the brim with freight and supplies.

Details about Clara's trip west are scarce. Since she was born into slavery, she had little opportunity to learn to read or write. No diary or letters about her journey have ever been found. It can safely be assumed that she cooked wild game and biscuits on the trail, as nearly all pioneer women did, and that she used common staples: salt pork and bacon to supplement the fresh game, hundreds of pounds of flour and sugar, rice, beans, baking soda, salt, and coffee. Most wagons carried water kegs as well. Clara's cooking gear might have included at least one large kettle, skillets, and a big coffee pot along with tin dishes and cups.

Although meals on the westward journey were usually plain and monotonous, women like Clara tried to add variety. Sometimes they formed cooked beans into a loaf that could be used as sandwich filler. If they found wild duck or goose eggs, they made simple cakes or custards. Some brought a few luxuries from home: canned oysters, pickles, or molasses. Others included dried fruit, vinegar, or wild berries to prevent

Clara Brown
THE DENVER PUBLIC LIBRARY, WESTERN HISTORY COLLECTION,
F-22858

scurvy. Being an experienced cook, Clara knew many tricks to create flavorful trail food. But her successes wouldn't have come without hardship. Pioneer women reported that their pots, which they suspended over the coals on forked sticks, regularly fell into the fire. Smoke irritated their eyes, and their backs ached from stooping over their cooking. Rain ruined their bread as they worked in the mud. Then came the tiring job of washing up. Hauling water was a never-ending chore.

Not every place along the trails had firewood for cooking, so women gathered "buffalo chips" to burn instead. After they overcame their initial disgust, they agreed the dried dung made very good fires and smudge pots for repelling mosquitos. Some families facing a long stretch without firewood tied sticks or logs under their wagons as reserve fuel. Others gathered sage and weeds to burn.

Like most pioneer women, Clara probably had only a few clothes, dark in color so they wouldn't show dirt. Washing clothes on the westward journey was a grueling job. Sometimes the wagons had to "lay over" a full day for laundering. If fuel was available, the women heated river or creek water in large kettles. If not, they scrubbed and rinsed clothes in cold water, using harsh soap that chapped their hands. Then they wrung out the garments and hung them on bushes or laid them on the grass to dry. By the trip's end their few dresses were threadbare. Many emigrant women were embarrassed about their coarse, patched clothing and were hesitant to be seen by visitors along the way. When icy winds struck they often didn't have enough outer clothes to keep warm. Their woven shawls were no match for the bitter elements.

It is thought that Clara's wagon company may have taken the Smoky Hill Trail from Leavenworth to Denver. This route followed the Kansas and Smoky Hill Rivers and then struck out across a dreaded stretch: the hot, dry, 120-mile expanse between the head of the Smoky Hill River and the Republican River in present-day Colorado. But when the wagons set out in April 1859, the weather would have been wet and cool, with spring rainstorms pounding down on the travelers. Rivers probably roared with run-off, making crossings terrifying and treacherous. Perhaps Clara had shoes to help her endure the cold mud, stones, and thorns under her feet, but perhaps not. Either way, she marched day after day along the banks of the rain-swollen Kansas River, and then up the Smoky Hill Valley, with the hope of finding her daughter.

As Clara's wagon train creaked and rattled along, the party would have encountered Cheyenne or Kiowa men and women. Clara felt empathy toward these native peoples whose lifestyle was threatened by the increasing flow of emigrants. She is said to have been part Cherokee herself and to have had a great understanding for people who were in difficulty. Clara insisted that all human beings were God's children.

As the weather turned warmer and then hot, the party would have approached the desert-like expanse between the two rivers and crossed the desolate area without adequate water or shade. Carrying plenty of full water kegs would make the wagons too heavy for the oxen to pull, so supplies were severely limited. Sometimes, as Clara made herself trudge along, she may have put a piece of dried apple under her tongue to keep her mouth moist. But a long, cool drink of clear water would have to wait.

If Clara's trip was like others on the Smoky Hill route, several days went by—endless, troubled, hot days—before the longed-for shout went up. The Republican River was in sight! They had crossed the worst, most dangerous stretch of trail. Now it was on to the gold camps of Colorado, still a part of Kansas Territory.

Clara must have seen new graves along the trail—the hard evidence of heartache and suffering in earlier wagon trains. When a person died, the others wrapped the body in a blanket and buried it beside the trail, usually marking the place with a pile of rocks or a homemade wooden cross.

As the wagons labored their way west, Clara probably yearned for a few minutes of quiet. All day long the cattle bawled. Men shouted instructions. The wagons creaked and groaned as the oxen's heavy hooves pounded the hard ground. Chains clanked, and iron wheels clattered over rocks. The canvas wagon covers snapped loudly in the wind.

Clara and the wagon train traveled northwest beyond the Republican River until the breathtaking Rocky Mountains rose in the distance.

Clara had never seen anything like them. They stood out against the deep blue sky, white snow glittering on their peaks. She looked forward to reaching the confluence of the South Platte River and Cherry Creek, where chokecherries were said to grow in abundance and the new twin towns of Auraria and Denver nestled. For now, she kept careful watch over the party's food supplies. After nearly eight weeks on the trail, the flour and sugar were probably getting low. The bacon and coffee were almost gone. But Clara somehow continued to feed the men until early June, when her party reached the small settlements.

She knew the gold camps were crowded with men living in harsh conditions who would gladly pay someone else to wash their clothes for them, and she planned to start a laundry service to support herself while she searched for her daughter. Soon after arriving in Denver, though, Clara found a job in a bakery and a small cabin in which to live. She settled in and began the task for which she is best remembered today: helping to establish Denver's first Sunday school. She gave her time generously to church work, offering the use of her cabin for services. People knew this kind, dedicated newcomer as "Aunt" Clara Brown.

Clara realized that a laundry service would be in greater demand in a more remote area. As much as she hated to leave her new friends, she hired a prospector to take her forty miles up into a rugged mountain mining camp soon known as Central City. There she settled down and began her laundry work. Historians believe she charged fifty cents (commonly paid in gold dust) to wash and iron a shirt. Business was good.

Everywhere she went, she asked about her daughter. No one seemed to know Eliza Jane's whereabouts. It didn't help that Clara probably wasn't certain of her daughter's last name, which would have changed every time Eliza Jane was sold to a new slaveholder. But Clara was not about to give up. She knew a more extensive search—and her many humanitarian projects—would take money. She worked hard, saved her gold dust, and bought several buildings in Denver, Central City, and surrounding settlements. After a few years Clara's holdings were sizeable.

Meanwhile, her Central City cabin became a makeshift hospital and church. She nursed sick or injured miners and contributed time and money to establish churches in the booming gulch town. She reportedly fed countless hot meals to destitute families by purposely making huge batches of soups or stews and then claiming she had overcooked and needed help using the extra.

After the Civil War ended, Clara knew that Eliza Jane must be free. She decided to go south to search for her, traveling this time by stagecoach and train. Historians believe that Clara went as far as Kentucky, where her daughter had been sold away from her, but could find no trace of Eliza Jane. Sadly, she prepared to return to Central City.

Even in the face of her disappointment, Clara noticed that many of her fellow former slaves in the South were now destitute. Newly freed, their prospects were bleak as they tried to overcome severe prejudice, little formal education, and homelessness. Clara yearned to help. If she could take a group with her to what was now the Territory of Colorado, she could find good jobs and housing for them. Using the money she had earned through her shrewd investments, she did just that. She paid the way across the plains for a group of men, women, and orphans, some of whom may have been friends or relatives. When they reached Colorado, Clara helped them settle into jobs and homes.

As Clara grew older her good works continued. When she was in her seventies, old age began to take its toll. It is thought that she developed a heart condition which limited her activities, and that her charitable works had used up most of her money. Several of her buildings had been destroyed by fire. Before long she was poor and unable to work. But Clara was sure God would care for her. She prayed that he would help find her beloved daughter.

It was then that a longtime friend in Denver, where the lower altitude was better for Clara's heart, is believed to have offered her a cottage to live in, free, for the rest of her life. Gratefully she accepted and left the Central City home where she'd lived for nineteen years. Soon after, she was named a certified member of the Society of Colorado Pioneers.

Accounts differ on what happened next. Some researchers speculate that, in 1882, Clara received a letter from an old friend who had moved to Council Bluffs, Iowa. This friend had met a widow in her early fifties named Mrs. Eliza Jane Brewer who remembered being sold away from her family long ago in Kentucky. After excitedly asking more questions, the friend felt sure that Mrs. Brewer was Clara's daughter. Clara thought she would burst with happiness. She made immediate plans to travel to Iowa by train, hoping her friend was right.

Early in March of 1882, Eliza Jane Brewer met Clara Brown at the Council Bluffs station. According to stories, the two instantly recognized each other and embraced with tears of joy. After years of searching and wondering, Clara could hardly believe she was reunited with her beloved daughter.

The two enjoyed a long, satisfying visit before Clara returned to Denver. There, surrounded by friends, she lived out the last few years of her life. It is believed that Eliza Jane and Eliza's grown daughter joined her there, and were with her when she died on October 23, 1885.

Clara's legacies will always be a part of American history. After her covered wagon trip across the plains, she became one of Colorado's best-loved pioneers, admired for her generosity and compassion. "Aunt" Clara brought the enduring value of selflessness to a primitive wilderness boomtown and is remembered for her genuine love for all human beings. From her humble beginnings Clara Brown built a memorable life of purpose.

Driving the Sheep
The Story of Martha Missouri Bishop Moore

"I thought if there is peace to be found in the world the heart that was humble might hope for it here."
—MARTHA MISSOURI BISHOP MOORE, PASSING BY
SCOTTS BLUFF, NEBRASKA TERRITORY, JUNE 30, 1860

A FIERCE MISSOURI WIND ROCKED THE COVERED WAGON AS TWENTY-two-year-old Martha Moore struggled to make dinner without stepping outside. The white canvas top whipped in the gale until she was afraid it would rip to pieces—or worse, fly off altogether, leaving her exposed to the elements.

Unwrapping a couple of hard biscuits, Martha wondered how the sheep were faring. Her new husband, James Preston Moore, had acquired 5,100 of the wooly creatures, which they were driving from Missouri to California. A small group of covered wagons traveled with them. Martha knew that the overland trip would be difficult enough without bringing along thousands of blundering sheep. Still, everyone said that once they reached California, they would find nothing but abundance and prosperity. Maybe it would be worth the journey's hardships.

Although naturally optimistic, Martha was well aware that the venture had started with missteps. The second day on the trail, May 3, 1860, some of the group's horses had escaped, and the men had spent hours hunting for them. Six days out, the drovers discovered they had left a thousand sheep behind at the first night's camping spot. They had gone back to find them now, as Martha and the others waited in the windstorm.

She didn't want to get out of the wagon. As small and slight as she was, she was sure the tempest would blow her away. The wind would wreak havoc with her already muddy dress and her long, dark hair, which she liked to pin neatly behind her neck, leaving soft "wings" to cover her ears. At least it wasn't pelting rain; earlier in the trip, a two-hour rainstorm had left her completely drenched, even though she'd hunched beneath the wagon cover.

She gave up on making dinner. The biscuits would have to do, along with water she had dipped from a passing creek. Martha reached for her little journal to record the day's events. Although she wrote faithfully in small, slanted script that stretched from one edge of the lined paper to the other, she didn't say much about the wagon company or give many details about her ambitious husband, even if her affection for him was clear. Her short daily entries focused on people they encountered, problems they endured, weather, the beauty of the landscape, and the company's mood. She often mentioned another couple, Samuel and Margaret ("Mag") Dicus, good friends who were traveling west with them. There were also several drovers and a couple of expensive sheep dogs to help.

As the wagons left Missouri and entered what would soon be the new state of Kansas, the spring weather turned warm. Martha found ripe gooseberries along the trail, a tasty addition to their meals. Since the party had started out late in the season, the prairie sun would soon be scorching. Sheep trains often delayed a few weeks out of deference to other travelers, because their close-cropped grazing left little forage for anyone following.

James had traveled overland to California at least once before and staked a claim near the upper Sacramento River. He had made an earlier attempt to drive a band of sheep there, but had experienced terrible losses. This time, he hoped to do better. To protect the animals against drowning at the many river crossings, he doubtless sheared them before leaving Missouri; otherwise their wool would get water-logged and heavy. Stream crossings were problematic anyway. "It is almost impossible to force sheep across water," Martha wrote. "They wont go by good or foul means."

While the wagons moved slowly over the Kansas prairie, Martha rejoiced in the countryside's beauty, which spoke to her of God. She loved the enormous skies, crimson sunsets, winding creeks, and miles of green, waving grass. One pleasant evening, she stopped tending camp to weave a cedar wreath—a gift for her friend Mag.

For much of the trip, though, the other travelers were out of sorts. More than once, Martha wrote that "everyone was mad as usual." Indeed, it would be hard not to be irritated at the endless hardships the party endured. Even Martha's cheerful nature was sorely tried when she and Mag spent hours one May afternoon washing clothes and laying them out to dry, only to find later that their hands and arms were painfully blistered from sunburn.

The group reached the bank of the Kaw (Kansas) River and waited there, hoping the drovers would be able to force the sheep into the current. The animals were "very contrary and there was no getting them across," Martha reported in her diary. After several frustrating attempts and delays, the men finally succeeded. The party pressed on to the small outpost of Fort Riley.

From there they followed the Republican River, heading north-west to reach the main Oregon-California Trail along the Platte River,

Martha Missouri Bishop Moore

and avoiding as many stream crossings as they could. Wind and rain were a relief from the heat as the group wended its way upstream, covering only ten to fifteen miles a day. Martha mentioned that May 31, nearly a month after they had started west, was a particularly hard day. Drizzling rain, the raw sight of a fresh grave alongside the trail, and seven more dead sheep dampened her mood. By then she was getting weary of the daily exposure to the elements, along with the animals' slow pace and continual bleating. Often she rode horseback rather than endure the wagon's constant jolting, enjoying the fresh prairie breeze on her face and the warm sun on her shoulders.

On June 1, 1860, Martha and James celebrated their first wedding anniversary. In a poetic mood, Martha wrote that her year of marriage had taken her through "life's sunniest vales" and mentioned the abundance of good fortune that had characterized her wedded life. She knew she was largely on her own for the trip west, though, since James's attention had to be split between the sheep and constant, laborious daily tasks.

The group soon left the Republican River and its ready water. They drove the huge band north to the next river, the Blue, and then on to the Platte, where they turned onto the main Oregon-California Trail, following it upstream to Fort Kearney in today's state of Nebraska. There, Martha purchased yard goods to make a new dress and comforted Mag, whom she found weeping from homesickness. Then they continued up the Platte, marveling over its shallow depth. The weather alternated between rainstorms and muggy heat, but the scenery was tranquil and beautiful. Martha described it as "one perfect scene of rural loveliness."

When the party reached the South Platte, it took an entire day to force the sheep across. The group then wound its way up the North Platte, making its usual plodding progress. They passed Courthouse Rock, Chimney Rock, and lovely Scotts Bluff, still traveling in today's state of Nebraska. Martha noted the Fourth of July in her journal, lamenting that the patriotic tune of "The Star-Spangled Banner" had been replaced by the sound of the "mad wind soughing and sighing through the sand hills." When they reached Fort Laramie in present-day Wyoming, James sold one thousand head of sheep and Martha eagerly wrote letters home.

In her journal she noted that she was concerned about the number of the animals that were dying, partly due to the poisonous plants and alkali water they encountered, and the "pitiless fury" of the rainstorms followed by unbearable mud. Mosquitoes plagued them. "Will this interminable travel never end?" Martha wrote. "But why complain?"

After traveling for a week through the Black Hills, Martha studied the view behind them, writing poignantly, "As I look back they rise with bristling ruggedness as if to shut out forever from my sight the home of my childhood and those friends whom I love so well." Her parents had given her the middle name Missouri, a constant reminder of the beautiful homeland she had left behind. With the Black Hills rising behind the wagons, she could no longer imagine she could see Missouri in the far distance.

On July 9 the party left the North Platte River country for good. A few days later, they reached the Sweetwater River and passed Independence Rock. Words failed Martha at Devil's Gate, where she was awestruck by the stunning cliffs and narrow, rocky cleft chiseled by the stream. Near there, she and Mag took a "ramble" over the mountains, possibly to see the carved names of earlier travelers in the stone, but also to escape the tedium and jostling of wagon travel. There were many wagon trains—and at least one other sheep train—traveling at the same time; the Moore party encountered some of them along the Sweetwater. Fresh fish and wild strawberries broke the monotony of their diet.

As the days wore on, the group turned onto the new and federally funded Lander Road in today's state of Wyoming and progressed into what is now Idaho. On early August mornings Martha found ice in her wash pan. The party was dreadfully weary but still had the last third of the demanding trail to conquer.

Lost horses were a constant problem. Martha's journal often mentioned that the men were out looking for the animals, which wandered off at every opportunity. On August 9, while the rest of the party waited in camp for the searchers to return, a small party of Shoshones or Bannocks approached and unexpectedly began shooting at the travelers. "Every cheek was blanched white as driven snow, and we were running everywhere to get out of the way," Martha wrote. She and Mag hid in some nearby willows until James sent word that the teams were ready. Then they made a swift, horrified escape. One of the teamsters, however, had been shot in the arm, thigh, and ankle and was sent ahead to Fort Hall for help.

While they were driving hard to get away, the Moores' wagon overturned. They were forced to stop and reload their belongings. Although they hurried, the reloading seemed to take forever. Martha was trembling and nearly sick with fear. From then on she worried about lingering in isolated country and she dreaded driving through canyons, where the thought of ambush filled her with terror.

Ten days later, worn out and bedraggled, the party reached Fort Hall. Colonel Marshall Saxe Howe cordially greeted the travelers. Martha and the others, feeling safe at last, enjoyed a feast of roast beef while listening to the fort's small band.

The party passed American Falls on the Snake River and continued over the rough country to the Humboldt River—"this river famous for frogs, Alkali & Indians," wrote Martha. Here the arduous trail, amassed fatigue, and constant anxiety made the journey grim. Despite her fear, Martha traded with friendly Shoshones for crucial fresh venison and fish.

As the travelers continued down the Humboldt, the sheep dwindled in number. They developed sore feet, slowing travel even more.

On top of that, predators stalked the herd, allowing the stockmen little sleep.

Martha was grimy, drained of energy, and barely hanging on to her optimism. Exhaustion and constant discomfort left her feeling vulnerable and edgy. The days dragged on. She was glad when they left the Humboldt River with its clouds of choking dust and rough roads.

September crept past. The weather deteriorated. Heat was replaced by rain and cold winds. The group pressed on through the desert country of present-day Nevada, stopping at every possible spring to water the animals.

A long stretch of night driving and a stony trail led the company into today's state of California. Martha's diary tells of her fatigue and despair. Despite her misery, though, on the last day of September she wrote hopefully: "Tomorrow we expect to get to Honey Lake and we will be coming out of the wilderness sure enough I for one will be very much rejoiced."

The next day, October 1, 1860, Martha's journal abruptly ended. The Honey Lake Valley was visible in the distance, but the last demanding mountain crossing was still to come. It is believed that the party took the Nobles route north of Mount Lassen to reach the upper Sacramento Valley. There, Martha and James settled at Reed's Creek, just south of today's city of Red Bluff, near present-day Vina. The two of them worked their ranch, caring for the hardy sheep and other livestock that had survived the punishing overland journey.

Amid the rich native grass and wild oats that nourished their animals, James and Martha thrived. In 1861 their first child, Nancy, was born, and five others—Lee, Martha, Guy, Fell, and Roy—followed over the next thirteen years. In 1870, Mag and Samuel Dicus, who had settled in adjacent Butte County, moved closer to their old friends.

Although their lives were full and busy, the Moores did not enjoy longevity. James died of a heart condition in 1880, on Martha's forty-third birthday. Sadly, and for unknown reasons, she followed him in death a few months later, leaving their children orphaned. The youngest was about six years old.

However brief their life in northern California, which was roughly twenty years, Martha Missouri Bishop Moore and James Preston Moore made lasting contributions to the new state they helped settle. Sheep—and the many sheep-raising families who established themselves there—played an important role in the area's growing economy. The Moore children grew up to live productive lives. Some stayed in northern California, where one daughter became a schoolteacher.

Perhaps the family's most lasting gift was Martha's concise and insightful journal. Little did she guess that her faithful entries would one day offer a valuable glimpse into the travails of a sheep train on the overland trails—and the cheerful young woman who made the journey her own.

Shock and Grief on the Overland Trail
The Story of Mary Peters Ringo

WHEN MARY RINGO THOUGHT ABOUT HER UPCOMING WAGON TRIP to California, she worried about her five children and the tiny baby growing quietly inside her. She had heard about the terrible dangers for youngsters on the overland trail. Some nights she lay awake fretting about dreaded cholera outbreaks, dysentery, or accidental campfire burns. The thought of her children drowning or getting crushed under the wagon wheels nearly made her heart stop.

Mary didn't worry as much about her strong husband, Martin Ringo. A former infantryman and a farmer, he was in his midforties—much older than most westward travelers. He knew how to take care of himself and his growing family. Although he was fighting tuberculosis, the family thought California's warm climate would make him well again.

Little did Mary know what lay ahead.

On May 18, 1864, the Ringo family set out from Liberty, Missouri. Their two sons, Johnny (fourteen) and Albert (ten), were old enough to get into real mischief on the trail. The little girls, Fanny Fern (seven), Mary Enna (four), and Mattie Bell (two), would require careful minding. Fortunately, Fanny could probably be trusted to keep little Mattie Bell and Mary Enna away from the campfire while Mary kept the family fed and clothed.

The Ringos took their two wagons across the Missouri River on a ferry and started along the Leavenworth Road in the new state of Kansas. This led straight to the well-worn Oregon Trail. Unlike many travelers, the Ringos did not choose between oxen or mules for pulling; they brought along both. Mules would haul the smaller wagon, oxen the larger. If and when the teams gave out, Martin could hitch the two wagons together and pull both using the strongest remaining animals. Along the trail they would often meet and part with other travelers, combining into larger trains for safety.

By June 10 the party had reached the Platte River, and two days later, Fort Kearney. Mary is believed to have driven the mule wagon; she spent her days guiding the long-eared animals along the trail. Green prairie grasses blew gracefully in the wind. White clouds scudded across the sky, and occasional rain fell, cooling the air. Inside the wagon her little girls played by the hour.

Mary was pregnant again, but if she was peaked or nauseated, she never mentioned it in the journal she kept of the trip. Writing about such a deeply personal matter was out of the question. Besides, there was no use complaining, even to herself. There was rarely time to rest on the trail. She had to care for her family whether she felt good or not.

Although she was disappointed when there were no letters awaiting them at Fort Kearney, Mary mailed her own correspondence and bought yard goods for a dress at nearby Kearney City, reporting that the cost was about the same as back home. She began to relax about the trip. So far the children were healthy, the road fairly good, and the animals strong. She and her husband were well-liked by fellow travelers and were making new friends along the way. On June 22 she wrote in her journal, "We are getting along very well."

It wasn't long, though, before things grew difficult. Mary continued to write faithfully, noting scattered cattle, heavy rain, and her own pounding headaches. Deep sand made pulling hard for the animals. There was a long delay crossing the South Platte River and the party fell behind schedule. Mosquitoes, Mary said, "just swarm all over the prarie, no one can sleep for them scarcely and we are all getting very tired." Wolves howled near the wagons at night.

By then, she was undoubtedly wind-burned and tan, even with her sunbonnet. Despite her diligence in washing clothes, which she wrote about on several occasions, the children were dirty and ragged. The once-white wagon cover was gray from blowing dirt and rain, and the animals were wearing down. Even her pleasant husband was exasperated when the mules ran off. They pressed on. As the July sun beat down, Mary focused on the beautiful landscape, which included Courthouse Rock, Chimney Rock, and Scotts Bluff, all in today's state of Nebraska. She wrote of the "bad road but grand scenery."

Just past Scotts Bluff, the wagon train mistook a party of friendly Plains Indians for hostile ones, and someone fired a shot at them. This was reported at the nearby fort, so when the travelers arrived, they were detained and fined for their wrongdoing. They forfeited enough flour, coffee, sugar, and bacon to compensate for the misconduct. Mary noted that the company was "glad to get off on those terms." They continued along the trail.

On July 25 Martin and Mary discovered that one of their oxen was sick. They immediately unyoked the animal, but it died within an hour. Apparently the Ringos had extras, because they traveled on, saddened but without delay. Their party joined with more wagon travelers due to reports of skirmishes with the native peoples and the resulting deaths of earlier travelers. This, Mary wrote, "keeps me so uneasy and anxious." On July 28 a man from their own party was confronted and three horses stolen. The group was tense and edgy.

Mary Peters Ringo
FROM THE AUTHOR COLLECTION OF DAVID JOHNSON,
JOHN RINGO, KING OF THE COWBOYS (UNIVERSITY OF NORTH TEXAS PRESS, 2008)

Then, on July 30, as the company was camped in a wide sage-brush meadow surrounded by low hills along the North Platte River in today's state of Wyoming, an unimaginable tragedy occurred.

Mary's journal tells of the horror: "And now Oh God comes the saddest record of my life for this day my husband accidentally shot himself and was buried by the wayside and oh, my heart is breaking."

Early that morning, Martin had climbed up on the wagon to search the horizon for danger. His gun went off accidentally, shooting him through the head. He died immediately. Mary and at least one of her children, Johnny, witnessed the terrible scene. They were sick with shock and grief. Mary wrote that if it hadn't been for the children, she would gladly have lain down and died with her husband. She prayed for the strength to endure the "anguish that is breaking my heart" and for God's help in raising the children alone.

Martin Ringo was buried near the trail. With help from the other travelers, she and the children said goodbye to their beloved husband and father. Mary wrote: "Oh, the agony of parting from that grave, to go and leave him on that hillside where I shall never see it more." The wagon train moved out the same day. A friend named William Davenport drove the mule wagon for Mary at first. He also wrote a letter reporting Martin's death to the newspaper in the Ringos' hometown of Liberty, Missouri, saying, "He was buried near the place he was shot in as decent a manner as possible with the facilities on the plains."

The next few days were nearly intolerable for Mary. Not only had she lost her beloved husband and helpmate, but her situation was dire. Widowed with five children, another baby on the way, and grief so overwhelming she was nearly incapacitated, she prayed hard for strength and guidance. Comforting the children as best she could, she struggled to cope.

Her journal may have been a source of solace, for she often wrote about how lonely and sad she felt. The women of the wagon train kindly visited her, and the men helped with the animals and heavy work. Mary appreciated their kindness but was weighed down with sorrow. She wrote, "Oh God help me to bear this hard trial."

When she couldn't sleep she stared into the darkness, summoning her courage. She tried to form a plan. Her sister Augusta lived in California with her husband. Mary decided to continue to Salt Lake City, sell the wagons and animals, and, with the children in tow, take a stagecoach to San Jose to join them.

It would be another month until the wagons reached Salt Lake. To Mary the time seemed interminable. Moving in a daze, she took care of daily tasks and wrote in her journal, some days jotting only a terse sentence or two. The party inched its way along the Sweetwater River, over South Pass, and west to the Green River and Fort Bridger, all in today's state of Wyoming. Mary fought grief, fatigue, and headaches, but she carried on, knowing her children were depending on her.

When they finally arrived in Salt Lake City, Mary was told that her wagons and animals were so worn down that they were worth practically nothing. She decided not to sell them. Hiring a driver, she and the children set out for San Jose with the tired oxen, mules, and battered wagons. By then it was early September.

The first day out, the family drank some bad water that made them all sick. Soon after, the mules nearly died of the same affliction. Mary rested the animals and purchased feed to build their strength. Progress was slow, with frequent stops to let the exhausted animals recover. She continued to write in her journal, focusing now on the critical availability of grass and water. The weather began to turn cool as they wound their way along the Central Overland Route into today's state of Nevada. This trail was a good shortcut from Salt Lake City to Carson City.

As October arrived Mary reported mountainous terrain and severe fatigue. Nearly at the end of her pregnancy, she struggled on. Her diary entries were brief, but her quiet desperation was evident in the short sentences. In Austin, Nevada, a primitive silver-mining town, the family stopped to rest. Mary's cousin, Charley Peters, and an acquaintance from back home lived there and offered their support, helping her dispose of one wagon and her worn-out oxen.

On Saturday, October 8, Mary's journal ended abruptly with these words: "We remain in Austin, Nev." Shortly afterward, her sixth child was born. But the family's troubles were not over. The baby boy was, according to family history, "terribly disfigured" and stillborn. One can only imagine Mary's distress as they laid the child to rest, a second tragedy to compound her dreadful grief.

Somehow, she gathered the strength to finish the journey to California. In later years Mary's youngest daughter, Mattie Bell (Ringo) Cushing, finished the story of the family's trip. Mattie had been only two years old when the Ringos traveled the overland trails, so she had no memories of her own. However, she wrote down the final account as her mother told it.

They traveled, possibly by stagecoach while son Johnny drove the mules and remaining wagon, to San Jose by way of San Francisco. In San Jose they gladly reunited with Mary's sister and brother-in-law, Augusta and Coleman Younger, who had a large stock-raising operation. Mary and her children moved into their carriage house, which had been rebuilt into a small home. They stayed for a year, while Mary regained her strength. Then they moved into town. Accounts differ, but Mary may have run a boarding house, while her two sons worked to help support the family and the girls attended school.

"I think she was the bravest woman I ever heard of—left as she was with five children to look after and to have everything else to attend to and in the condition she was in," Mattie Bell Cushing wrote in hindsight.

Years later, Mary's older son became the famous outlaw and cattle rustler Johnny Ringo. Historians surmise that witnessing his father's shocking death and the death of his baby brother may have contributed to his life's path.

Mary Peters Ringo survived one of the most heartbreaking journeys on the overland trails. Drawing on her faith and reserves of inner strength, she battled overwhelming grief and fear to get her children safely to California. There, near her sister, she began a new life that would always be colored—but not defeated—by her traumatic trip west.

With Determined Optimism
The Story of Sarah Raymond

TWENTY-FIVE-YEAR-OLD SARAH RAYMOND RODE TO THE TOP OF A green bluff on her bay pony. Below her a small group of covered wagons made its slow way west across the Iowa plains. Holding her sunbonnet in her hand, she waved merrily to her friends and family.

Sarah watched the two wagons she shared with her mother and grown brothers that summer of 1865. Her father had died several years before. There was a large, heavy wagon to haul household goods, as well as a lighter spring wagon to carry everyday items and provide a sleeping place for the two women. Sarah could even see their churn filled with this morning's heavy cream fastened to the freight wagon. The day's steady lurching would turn the cream into soft butter in time for the family to enjoy it on their homemade bread for supper.

Nearby were the four wagons belonging to the large Kerfoot family, their neighbors from back home in Sand Hill, Missouri. Sarah's gentle friend Neelie would be riding in one, perhaps mending clothes for her younger sisters and brothers. What a sweet, helpful person she was! Sarah had been trying to teach Neelie how to cook over a campfire. Preparing food for a family of twelve was no easy task, even for an experienced cook. And the Kerfoot women were not experienced. At home servants had always prepared their meals. Neelie's biscuits were hard and dry, but she cheerfully kept trying to learn the art of baking in a sheet iron camp stove. She doggedly brought the refinements of home to the trail by polishing the family's tin dishes until they gleamed, and by putting out a bouquet of flowers with each evening meal.

Sarah urged her pony down from the bluff and hurried to catch up to the passing wagons. She wasn't afraid of riding alone in this wild country, often taking solitary rides for recreation. She had a strong faith that God would watch over her. Her mother, though, was concerned about the many dangers surrounding them and preferred that her daughter stay near the group.

In Sarah's mind it had been a glorious trip so far. Her buoyant spirits could not be dampened by cold rain, mud, or even swarms of biting mosquitoes. She happily told friends, "It is so jolly to be going across the continent; it is like a picnic every day for months; I was always sorry picnic days were so short, and now it will be an all Summer picnic." When the young men of the train hung a home-made swing from a low-hanging tree limb, Sarah (or "Miss Sallie," as she was fondly nicknamed) was the first to soar high into the leafy branches. Careful to help her mother with the trail work, she also took time to climb nearby landmarks for spectacular vistas, or to appreciate the beauty of an approaching storm. She regularly visited her friends, especially Neelie.

Later she would be glad she had.

Before leaving Missouri on May 1, 1865, Sarah had promised friends she would keep a journal of her trip west, so she carefully wrote down each day's events. Her wagon-train friends teased her gently about this, but her mother felt Sarah's writing was a gift to be nurtured. Mrs. Raymond willingly did much of the evening work so Sarah would have time to record their trip. Many years after their westward journey was over, Sarah's diary was published.

Sarah Raymond
MONTANA HISTORICAL SOCIETY RESEARCH CENTER

By the mid-1860s, when Sarah and her family were traveling, rela-
tions between white travelers and the native tribes of the West had
become explosive. Conflicts often resulted in deaths along the trails.

The US government had established new military posts on the western routes and requested that emigrants travel in groups of forty to sixty wagons for protection. Wagon trains were to camp near each other if possible. To obey these new orders, the Raymonds' small party joined a much larger wagon train in Nebraska soon after crossing the Missouri River. The Hardinbrooke Train, as it was called, would stay together until the group had passed through today's Colorado and most of Wyoming.

In spite of the fear and hostility that existed between the travelers and the native peoples—discussed openly in Sarah's dairy—there were no violent encounters on the Raymonds' trip, although they saw grisly evidence of several conflicts. Each night, the wagon train formed a tight circle and corralled the animals inside. Men took turns guarding the camp, and the Raymonds' watchdog, Caesar, slept under their wagon. The group traveled close to other large trains.

Everyone liked Sarah. Time after time she helped those who were sick or trail weary. As the wagons snaked across the wide prairie, she nursed fellow travelers, babysat a child whose mother was ill, drove the horse team that pulled the spring wagon, and comforted those who were discouraged. She generously shared her sleek pony with friends and family when she realized that jolting along in a hard wagon all day was exhausting.

The unmarried gentlemen did not fail to notice Sarah's thoughtful, sunny nature. Many times, one young man or another asked to walk with her in the moonlight or accompany her on a horseback ride. They gave her candy, bouquets of wildflowers, and sweet red apples. Sarah appreciated the gifts and friendship but seemed in no hurry to become attached. She was independent and self-sufficient. At the age of fourteen, she had earned her teaching certificate—something that was possible for a diligent student at that time—and had already taught school for several years.

Mrs. Raymond, Sarah, and her two brothers—eighteen-year-old Winthrop and twenty-year-old Hillhouse—soon faced a decision that would affect the rest of their lives. When they left Missouri, they hadn't decided upon a destination. They knew only that they were going west to better their circumstances. California's sunny winters beckoned, but so did Oregon's lush valleys and the gold discoveries in Montana Territory. Finally, they chose Montana, turning their thoughts to the well-known gold camp of Virginia City. Sarah hoped they could persuade Neelie's family to join them, but feared the Kerfoots would choose to settle in California instead.

Sarah was surprised at how many people were going west that year. But the bitter Civil War had just ended. Southerners and Northerners alike were weary and heavyhearted. Some, like Mr. Kerfoot, believed that the government was going to collapse. Thousands were ready for a new life in a new place.

On July 1 the party reached Colorado's South Platte River along with neighboring wagon trains. Sarah drove the spring wagon across the half-mile-wide ford. The next day, as her group camped with others on the north bank of the river, she marveled at the huge number of wagons, animals, and people that sprang up overnight.

Although the wagons were able to ford the South Platte, by 1865 westward travelers were sometimes forced to cross shaky toll bridges. The bridge keepers would block off easy fording places with large logs or ditches, so there was no choice but to use the bridge and pay the toll. Usually it was fifty cents or a dollar per wagon. Sarah reported with exasperation many such bridges on their trip.

On July 4 the dusty wagons stopped for a few hours in a shady grove of cottonwoods. To celebrate the holiday, the families ate savory roast antelope with oyster dressing and even cake and custard, carefully made with the last of the fresh eggs they had preserved in salt.

Sarah's diary tells of picking native gooseberries and gathering wild onions. Perhaps she, like some pioneer women, rolled out a pie crust on the wagon seat and baked a gooseberry pie over glowing coals. One hot afternoon near Elk Mountain, one of Sarah's brothers found a small patch of sheltered snow. Sarah took delight in eating a snowball. Another day she wrote about watching a prairie dog colony. In the evenings she and her friends gathered, probably around a crackling campfire, for guitar music and singing.

Near the crossing of the North Platte River in today's Wyoming, a note of anxiety crept into Sarah's writing. Neelie was sick. Sarah wrote: "Neelie continues to drag around; she will not acknowledge that she is sick enough to go to bed, but she certainly looks sick."

Neelie had good days and bad. Sometimes she felt better, but other times she was feverish and weak. Finally, in late July, she came to her friend for help. Sarah wrote:

> *I was sitting in mother's camp-chair idling and thinking, when Neelie came to me. She dropped upon the grass beside me and, laying her head in my lap, said, "Oh, Miss Sallie, I am afraid I am going to be sick in spite of everything, and I have tried so hard to get well without sending for the doctor."*

The wagon company was fortunate to have with them Dr. Fletcher, a young physician who had taken a liking to Neelie. Sarah helped put the girl to bed and then called for him, knowing he would offer Neelie his best care.

The group pressed on. Each bump jostled Neelie as she lay in her bed. Sarah, riding her pony nearby, wondered if the Kerfoot family's poor, monotonous diet had made Neelie sick. But Dr. Fletcher and another physician, Dr. Howard, who was soon called from a neighboring wagon train, agreed that she had mountain fever. This was most likely typhoid, which causes high fever, headache, and stiff muscles. The doctors agreed Neelie might get better if her family stopped for a few days to allow her to rest. But as much as Mr. Kerfoot loved his sweet, unselfish daughter, he was afraid of the dangers facing a solitary family, and he decided it was best to keep up with the rest of the train. They continued along the grueling trail. Sarah stayed beside her friend, giving her medicine and watching over her at the risk of catching mountain fever herself. Even with Sarah's tender care, however, Neelie continued to get worse.

By then Mr. Kerfoot had made a firm decision to settle in California. Up ahead, Sarah knew, was the split in the road where the wagons bound for Montana Territory and those heading to California would part company. She dreaded the day when she would have to leave her friend.

On July 27 the wagon train divided into two parts in preparation for the fork in the trail. As she watched the Kerfoot wagons join the California-bound company, Sarah took comfort in the fact that for the next few days, until they reached the fork, the two parties would travel near each other. She was sure she would see her friend again.

On Saturday, August 5, Neelie's cousin Frank from the California train galloped up to Sarah's party and asked Dr. Fletcher to come see the sick girl immediately. Sarah followed, hoping to see her, too. Frank described Neelie as "delirious" and "too weak to talk."

When they arrived at the Kerfoot wagon train, Sarah was profoundly disappointed. The doctor felt any excitement at all might make Neelie worse. It was decided that seeing Sarah would excite her too much. Sadly, Sarah agreed and returned to her own wagon train.

All too soon, the Raymonds' party turned north. Sarah wrote these heart-wrenching lines in her diary: "I feel the parting with our friends so distressingly. It is not likely we will meet again in this life." Each day in her prayers she remembered her friend traveling in pain and fever along the rough trail to California, and almost certainly Sarah must have asked the family to write her in Virginia City about Neelie's health.

Sarah felt it was her duty to stay cheerful. As saddened as she was by the recent happenings, she kept up her brave outlook while the small group wound its way north through rugged Idaho. She reported a variety of daily events: curing a sick ox by feeding him melted lard and bacon, meeting a spunky ninety-three-year-old woman traveling with another wagon party, tracking down a stolen horse, and taking long rides on her pony. Her group followed mountain trails so steep that Sarah wondered if the wagons "would turn a somersault" coming down. Some days they went fishing and ate their plentiful catch for breakfast.

Sarah quietly worried about Neelie, but another concern bothered her, too. The Raymonds had used up much of their money replenishing supplies and paying tolls. They would need more once they reached Virginia City. Several people had offered to buy Sarah's well-fed, healthy pony, but she had always refused. Now, as they neared their destination, she felt that she ought to sell him to help her family. Unwilling to do it herself, she asked her brother Hillhouse to accept a generous offer of $125 in gold dust. After the gentle pony was gone, Sarah couldn't stop her tears.

On September 1 the party entered what is now Montana. When Sarah awoke the next morning and peeked out of the wagon, soft snow glimmered on the surrounding mountains. A few days later, on September 5, Mrs. Raymond, Sarah, Winthrop, and Hillhouse arrived at the dirty, bustling mining town of Virginia City. Sarah wrote: "It is the shabbiest town I ever saw, not a really good house in it. Hillhouse and I, after hunting up and down the two most respectable looking streets, found a log cabin with two rooms that we rented for eight dollars per month." Letters were waiting for them at the post office. One was from Neelie's cousin, Frank.

Sarah's heart must have faltered when she saw it. The letter contained the bad news she had feared: Neelie had died. Shortly after the wagons had separated—following a long, hot, dusty day of traveling—Neelie had fallen into what her father thought was peaceful sleep. Every effort was made, but no one could wake her. The next morning she took her last breath.

From faraway in the gold camp, Sarah grieved deeply. For the first time she wrote in her journal about being homesick. But with her typical fortitude, she tried to make the best of the situation. She cleaned the cabin—which had a dirt roof—and took in sewing to earn money. It wasn't long before she became Virginia City's schoolteacher.

Teaching in the primitive town was not easy. Sarah had schoolchildren of all ages, as well as an odd assortment of textbooks brought to the gold camp by one family or another. With these meager supplies, she patiently set to work to teach her young students to read and write.

Sarah probably taught in Virginia City for just one year, because on May 27, 1867, she married thirty-four-year-old James M. Herndon, a carpenter and miner who later operated a furniture store in Virginia City. Sarah became a homemaker and Sunday school teacher. She and James eventually had five children. The family spent many years in Montana.

Sarah Raymond Herndon always remembered her four-month-long covered wagon trip to Montana Territory. Her journey was made remarkable by her cheerful outlook in the face of hardship. With determined optimism, she brightened her fellow travelers' darkest moments, making the difficult trip seem more like the summer picnic she imagined than the desolate journey many covered wagon travelers experienced.

A Honeymoon Trip to Montana
The Story of Ellen Louisa Gordon Fletcher

ELLEN FLETCHER LEANED BACK IN HER COVERED WAGON'S COMFORT-able armchair. Through the opening in the white canvas overhead, she could see a perfect rainbow glowing against the gray Wyoming sky. The enticing smells of frying bacon and wood smoke drifted into the cozy wagon. Billy was cooking breakfast again. For a few moments she snuggled inside her woolen shawl, warm and contented.

To twenty-five-year-old Ellen (known to her family as "Nellie"), this 1866 honeymoon trip to Montana Territory's famous gold camp, Virginia City, was the experience of a lifetime. She was a New York schoolteacher who had met thirty-seven-year-old William Asbury Fletcher when he fell ill during a trip east from the Montana mining towns. He had started a butcher shop near Virginia City and wanted to return. Ellen nursed him back to health, and the two had married in April 1866.

Shortly after their wedding, they left New York by train, later tak-ing a steamer up the Missouri River to Bellevue, Nebraska. From there they continued the journey to Montana Territory by covered wagon on the Old Mormon Trail. The long trip up the north bank of the Platte River went well. Beyond Fort Laramie, in the southeast corner

Ellen Louisa Gordon Fletcher
COURTESY OF GANDEE PRINTING CENTER, INC.

of today's state of Wyoming, they turned off onto the new and dangerous Bozeman Trail.

The "Bloody Bozeman" was indeed a hazardous route for settlers
to take. The Sioux nation had recently conquered the surrounding territory from the Crow people and considered it prime hunting grounds.

But the US Congress wanted this comparatively short, easy route to the Montana gold fields open to settlers and suppliers.

Bloodshed resulted.

Even when she saw evidence of warfare, though, Ellen felt safe. Her new husband, whom she affectionately called Billy, was a strong, capable traveler who could afford the necessities of the long journey. He had prepared for the trip with well-built wagons, hardy mules, and hundreds of pounds of supplies—including five hundred pounds of flour alone.

Certain that their healthy animals could handle the heavy load, the Fletchers had added a few luxuries to make the trip more pleasant. Before leaving Nebraska they purchased three pretty, fabric-bottomed folding chairs, including an armchair for the wagon. Along with the ordinary food staples, they carried four dozen cans of peaches as well as oysters, blackberry wine, and syrup. There was vinegar and molasses, and dried fruit (apples, peaches, currants, and prunes) to go with their supplies of codfish, bacon, and ham. They even brought their opera glass for looking at distant objects.

Ellen watched the rainbow fade from the sky. She could hear the soft voices of Billy's sister, Chell (Rachel), and his daughter from an earlier marriage, Ella, outside. There were other sounds, too. A jay in the scrubby undergrowth called to the campers. Horses nickered. Others in the train of twenty-five wagons were hitching up or preparing coffee over snapping fires. Once in a while, Ellen could hear her brother Will and Billy's brother Townie taking care of the mules.

As she pulled her long dress and warm shawl closer, perhaps Ellen wondered if she was already expecting a child. She and Billy had been married about two months, and she had been feeling rather tired lately. It was nice that he made the morning fire and breakfast, letting her sleep. Such kindness was typical of him. In fact, the whole Fletcher group had traveled in harmony, sharing the chores and doing small courtesies for each other since they'd left the banks of the Missouri in May.

Ellen straightened up the wagon. Before stepping into the crisp, pungent morning air for breakfast and coffee with her husband, she sat down and penciled a few lines in her small leather-covered diary, beginning with her usual Scripture verse. Later in the day she would add to the long letter she was writing to her family back home.

The route they were traveling had a short but violent history of conflict. Despite the angry Sioux, who considered wagon travelers invaders into their pristine hunting territory, emigrants continued to use it. In addition to the plentiful grass and water for livestock, the Bozeman Trail was roughly four hundred miles shorter than the alternate route.

The Fletchers' timing was fortunate. Just when their party (which had joined a larger wagon train to increase their numbers) turned onto the Bozeman Trail, US government agents had gathered at Fort Laramie to make a treaty with the Sioux. The treaty would officially open the trail to emigrants. Although many tribal leaders refused to attend the council, charging that the government intended to open the route with or without their consent, most were clustered near the fort. The Fletcher party slipped over the Bozeman Trail while the Sioux were thus otherwise occupied. Earlier and later Bozeman Trail travelers encountered the tribe's fury. Only two years later, led by Chief Red Cloud, the Sioux triumphed in closing the trail and the new military forts along the route.

Ellen wrote with fascination, but without fear, about the hundreds of native people they did encounter on the trip. Their ways intrigued her, and she conversed comfortably with them, once trading a cup of sugar for a pair of beaded moccasins. She asked to see the long ornaments they wore in their ears, later describing the bright-colored beads and shells fastened to the ends. Once she watched the women put up tepees, writing home that the lodges were "made of elk skins nicely pieced together, and looked very novel and pretty to me, with the poles sticking out of the top."

Ellen's enthusiastic letters reflected her congenial, lighthearted spirit. She and Billy were happy, the traveling—although difficult—was exciting, and new sights greeted her daily. She wrote page after page, especially to her sisters whom she missed terribly, painting word pictures like her description of one night's camp:

It was a pretty sight, the circular correll of white topped wagons and tents scattered here and there, the blazing fires shining through the trees, the busy men and women hurrying to and fro, and the quiet moon looking down over it all. A large tree, bent over like an arch, crowns our wagon. I could'nt help wishing that you could overlook the scene.

She wrote that her husband brought her pretty bouquets of wild-flowers, and told of enjoying hot, savory oyster soup and roast antelope for supper. Other times, she described the awe-inspiring scenery, inviting her family to join them out West. Often she enclosed flowers she'd pressed along the route, tiny chips of colorful agate, or later, sparkling flecks of Virginia City gold.

While her letters usually bubbled with enthusiasm, Ellen sometimes elaborated on the less pleasant aspects of the journey in her diary. The weather was freezing cold or unbearably hot, and the road was bad enough to break the wagon axles, causing delays. She told of mosquito swarms, irritating burrs that stuck to her clothing, and a dreadful toothache Billy endured. In one shaken paragraph she mentioned that her capable husband nearly drowned at a dangerous stream crossing, but was rescued by other travelers who threw ropes to him. And she was distressed when, contrary to her beliefs as a devout Methodist, it was necessary to work or travel on the Sabbath.

The group pressed on, crossing the Powder, Tongue, Big Horn, and Yellowstone Rivers in today's Wyoming and southern Montana. Ellen sometimes rode in the wagon, but other times walked or rode horseback. She admired the green mountain valleys and the rushing streams, writing that this was "the finest country I have ever yet seen." Groups of Arapaho and Cheyenne clustered around the wagons, wanting to trade. The trail was so steep in places that some emigrants actually switched the wheels on their wagons, putting the two large back wheels on the downhill side and the smaller front wheels on the uphill side to prevent rollovers. Teams were doubled. Ellen reported walking over the final perpendicular, washed-out stretch of road that led, at last, to Virginia City. They arrived on July 27, 1866.

In her letters Ellen described the far-flung little town, with its surrounding stripped hills and ugly diggings. She also mentioned the "very fine stone buildings, quite stylish and city-like" and the smallest houses she had ever seen—which reminded her of chicken coops— "built right on the mountain side."

After a few days they continued several miles up into the mountains to another gold camp, site of the butcher shop Billy had established earlier with his brother Townie. There they found a two-room cabin to live in while Billy began building a log house. He chose a spot on a steep mountainside where the view, according to Ellen, was "splendid." From her temporary cabin she watched the miners prospecting for gold with their sluice boxes. She was amused by their bachelor lifestyle. Most lived in tiny makeshift huts and ate bakery-purchased pies and meat on a stick. She said that some of the men were "real gentlemen," despite their reputation for drinking and carousing.

For entertainment she sifted through the mine tailings to find small semi-precious garnets, and visited with other women of the settlement. When Billy finished their log house, they moved in. Ellen described their rustic handmade furniture and warm feather beds and pillows. Food prices were high, but it seems as though they had supplies left over from the trip and enough money to buy what they needed.

On March 5, 1867, Ellen and Billy's first child, Blanche Montana Fletcher, was born. Ellen had, after all, been expecting her baby on the wagon journey, but like most pioneer women was reserved about discussing such private matters in her diary.

Typically, gold camps had short lives. Before long the initial mining boom in Virginia City and the adjacent camps began to fade. Billy and Townie decided to ranch in the warmer nearby Madison Valley. There they built another snug log house and a stable on the golden rangeland surrounded by purple mountains. Ellen joined them, and eventually this beautiful valley with its sweeping vistas became their permanent home.

Little Blanche delighted her parents. During the following years she was joined by several younger brothers and sisters. Ellen and Billy ranched, made and sold butter, taught Sunday school, continued the butchering business, and raised their large family in the cradle of the Madison Valley. One of Ellen's letters tells of riding "well wrapped up with blankets and buffalo robes" to a neighboring ranch to celebrate Christmas. For many years the warm, busy Fletcher home was a favorite stop for friends and customers alike. Today, the family is remembered for being true Montana pioneers.

Ellen Louisa Gordon Fletcher was a literate, adventurous young woman when she passed over the Bozeman Trail. She carefully recorded the details of her trip, which became lifelong memories and a treasured heritage to pass down to her children and grandchildren. A devoted mother and a sunny, descriptive writer, Ellen became a historian in her own way. With her detailed writings she put down on paper forever her rare account of what it was like to be a bride on the Bozeman Trail.

BIBLIOGRAPHY

Specific Sources for Sarah Eleanor Bayliss Royce's Story

Editors of Time-Life Books with text by Joan Swallow Reiter. The Old West Books. *The Women.* New York: Time-Life Books, 1979.

Levy, Joann. *They Saw the Elephant: Women in the California Gold Rush.* Hamden, CT: Archon Books, an imprint of Shoe String Press, 1990.

National Geographic Society. *Trails West.* Washington, DC: National Geographic Society, Special Publications Division, 1979.

Royce, Sarah. *A Frontier Lady: Recollections of the Gold Rush and Early California.* Lincoln: University of Nebraska Press, 1977. (Reprint of the 1932 edition by Yale University Press.)

Specific Sources for Tabitha Moffatt Brown's Story

Brown, Tabitha Moffatt. The "Brimfield Heroine" letter, August 1854, as published in *Covered Wagon Women: Diaries and Letters from the Western Trails, 1840–1849,* edited and compiled by Kenneth L. Holmes, vol. 1. Glendale, CA: Arthur H. Clark, 1983.

Pringle, Virgil K. "Journal of Virgil K. Pringle: Crossing the Plains in 1846." Manuscript copy. Pacific University Archives, Harvey W. Scott Memorial Library, Forest Grove, Oregon.

Read, Richard T. "The Early Days of Pacific University." Pacific University, Forest Grove, Oregon.

Spooner, Ella Brown. *Tabitha Brown's Western Adventures.* New York: Exposition Press, 1958.

Specific Sources for Amelia Stewart Knight's Story

Clark County Pioneers: A Centennial Salute. Vancouver, WA: Clark County Genealogical Society, 1989, pp. 406–409.

Eide, Ingvard Henry, ed. and photog. *Oregon Trail.* Chicago: Rand McNally, 1972.

Knight, Amelia. Pioneer diary as published in *Covered Wagon Women: Diaries and Letters from the Western Trails, 1853–1854,* edited and compiled by Kenneth L. Holmes, vol. 6. Glendale, CA: Arthur H. Clark, 1986.

Specific Sources for Mary Rockwood Powers's Story

Malone, Michael P., ed. *Historians and the American West.* Lincoln: University of Nebraska Press, 1983.

Powers, Mary Rockwood. *A Woman's Overland Journey to California.* Fairfield, WA: Ye Galleon Press, 1985.

Powers, W. P., comp. *Some Annals of the Powers Family.* Los Angeles, CA, 1924.

Specific Sources for Julia Anna Archibald's Story

Archibald (Holmes), Julia Anna. Pioneer letters as published in *Covered Wagon Women: Diaries and Letters from the Western Trails, 1854–1860*, edited and compiled by Kenneth L. Holmes, vol. 7. Glendale, CA: Arthur H. Clark, 1988.

Grant, Bruce. *Famous American Trails.* Chicago: Rand McNally, 1973.

Lavender, David. *Bent's Fort.* Garden City, NY: Doubleday, 1954.

Spring, Agnes Wright. *A Bloomer Girl on Pike's Peak 1858.* Denver: Western History Department, Denver Public Library, 1949.

Specific sources for Clara Brown's Story

Bruyn, Kathleen. *"Aunt" Clara Brown: Story of a Black Pioneer.* Boulder, CO: Pruett, 1970.

Katz, William Loren. *Black Women of the Old West.* New York: Atheneum Books for Young Readers, 1995.

Pelz, Ruth. *Black Heroes of the Wild West.* Seattle, WA: Open Hand, 1990.

Specific Sources for Martha Missouri Bishop Moore's Story

Butterfield, Ira H., Jr. "Michigan to California in 1861." *Michigan History Magazine,* July 1927: pp. 392–423.

Hitchcock, Ruth Hughes. *Leaves of the past, 1828–1880: a pioneer register, including an overview of the history and events of early Tehama County.* Chico, CA: Association for Northern California Records and Research, 1980.

Moore, Martha Missouri Bishop. *Journal of a trip to California, 1860.* Yale University Beinecke Library, Frontier Women microfilm set WA MSS-S1438, vol. 1 partial.

Moore, Martha Missouri Bishop. Pioneer diary (*Journal of a trip to California, 1860*) as published in *Covered Wagon Women: Diaries and Letters from the Western Trails, 1854–1860*, edited and compiled by Kenneth L. Holmes, vol. 7. Glendale, CA: Arthur H. Clark, 1988.

"Nobles Trail," Trails West: Marking the Emigrant Trails to California, 2010. http://emigranttrailswest.org/virtual-tour/nobles-trail/. Accessed April 2016.

"Trail Facts," Oregon-California Trails Association, 2016. www.octa-trails.org/learn/trail-facts. Accessed March 2016.

Wentworth, Edward Norris. *America's Sheep Trails: History, Personalities.* Ames: Iowa State College Press, 1948.

Specific Sources for Mary Peters Ringo's Story

"Central Overland Trail," Family Search Research Wiki, 2016 Intellectual Reserve. https://familysearch.org/wiki/en/Central_Overland_Trail. Accessed May 2016.

Johnson, David D. *John Ringo, King of the Cowboys: His Life and Times from the Hoo Doo War to Tombstone.* 2nd ed. Denton: University of North Texas Press, 2008.

"Mary Peters Ringo," Geni.com, 2016. www.geni.com/people/Mary-Peters -Ringo/6000000004570267353#. Accessed April 2016.

"National Historic Trails Auto Tour Route Interpretive Guide across Nevada," National Park Service, National Trails Intermountain Region, April 2012. www.nps.gov/poex/planyourvisit/upload/NevadaATR-IG-041612_web .pdf. Accessed May–June 2016.

Ringo, David Leer. *The Millennium Library Edition of the Ringo Family History Series: An Insert for the Third Printing.* Utica, KY: McDowell, 2002.

Ringo, Mary Peters. Pioneer diary (*The 1864 Journal*) as published in *Covered Wagon Women: Diaries and Letters from the Western Trails, 1862–1865*, edited and compiled by Kenneth L. Holmes, vol. 8. Spokane, WA: Arthur H. Clark, 1989.

Specific Sources for Sarah Raymond's Story

Griffith, H. Winter, M.D. *Complete Guide to Symptoms, Illness, & Surgery.* Tucson, AZ: Body Press, a division of HP Books, 1985.

Raymond, Sarah. *Days on the Road: Crossing the Plains in 1865.* New York: Burr Printing House, 1902.

Settle, Raymond W., and Mary Lund, eds. *Overland Days to Montana in 1865: The Diary of Sarah Raymond and Journal of Dr. Waid Howard.* Glendale, CA: Arthur H. Clark, 1971.

World Book Encyclopedia. Chicago: World Book, 1990.

Specific Sources for Ellen Louisa Gordon Fletcher's Story

Fletcher, Ellen. The Ellen (Nellie) Fletcher Papers, 1866–1870: Small Collection 78. Helena: The Montana Historical Society Archives.

Haines Jr., Francis D., ed. *A Bride on the Bozeman Trail: The Letters and Diary of Ellen Gordon Fletcher, 1866.* Medford, OR: Gandee Printing Center, 1970.

Johnson, Dorothy M. *The Bloody Bozeman: The Perilous Trail to Montana's Gold.* New York: McGraw-Hill, 1971.

Madison County History Association, comps. *Pioneer Trails and Trials: Madison County 1863–1920.* Ennis, MT: Madison County History Association, 1976.

Sievert, Ken and Ellen. *Virginia City and Alder Gulch.* Helena: Montana Magazine and American & World Geographic Publishing, 1993.

Additional Sources

Brown, Dee. *The Gentle Tamers: Women of the Old Wild West.* Lincoln: University of Nebraska Press, 1981. (Originally published New York: Putnam, 1958.)

Editors of Time-Life books with text by Joan Swallow Reiter. The Old West Books. *The Women.* New York: Time-Life Books, 1979.

Editors of Time-Life Books with text by Huston Horn. The Old West Books. *The Pioneers.* New York: Time-Life Books, 1976.

Faragher, John Mack. *Women and Men on the Overland Trail.* New Haven, CT: Yale University Press, 1979.

Holmes, Kenneth L., ed. and comp. *Covered Wagon Women: Diaries and Letters from the Western Trails 1840–1890,* vols. 1-11. Glendale, CA, 1983–88, and Spokane, WA, 1989–93: Arthur H. Clark.

Myres, Sandra L. *Westering Women and the Frontier Experience, 1800–1915.* Albuquerque: University of New Mexico Press, 1982.

National Geographic Society, Special Publications Division. *Trails West.* Washington, DC: National Geographic Society, 1979.

Ross, Nancy Wilson. *Westward the Women.* New York: Alfred A. Knopf, 1944.

Schlissel, Lillian. *Women's Diaries of the Westward Journey.* New York: Schocken Books, 1982.

Museums
Clark County Historical Museum, Vancouver, Washington.
End of the Oregon Trail Interpretive Center, Oregon City, Oregon.
National Historic Trails Interpretive Center, Casper, Wyoming.
Old College Hall Museum, Pacific University, Forest Grove, Oregon.
Old Fort Hall Replica, Pocatello, Idaho.

Audio/Visual
In Search of the Oregon Trail. Producer/director Michael Farrell. PBS
documentary, April 1996. Co-produced by Oregon Public Broadcasting
and the Nebraska ETV Network.

Maps
"California Trail Map of Routes," Ancestry.com, 1997–2016. http://freepages
.history.rootsweb.ancestry.com/~fgsiler/Migration%20Photo%20
Galleries/(9)%20PACIFIC%20COAST/PACIFIC%20COAST%20
(GEN%20MAPS)/CaliforniaTrailMapofRoutes.pdf. Accessed
January–March 2016.
"Map of 4-Trails Feasibility Study Trail Routes," National Park Service,
National Trails Intermountain Region. www.nps.gov/cali/learn/
management/upload/4-TrailsFS_Map_032411_sm.pdf. Accessed
March 2016.
The Oregon Trail: Transforming the West, 5th ed., 1995. Produced by the Oregon
Trail Coordination Council. Karen Bassett, illustrator. Jim Johnston,
American Adventures Press, producer.
Western Emigrant Trails 1830–1870: Major Trails, Cutoffs, and Alternates, 2nd
ed., 1991, 1993. Published by the Oregon-California Trails Association.
Robert L. Berry, map project editor. James A. Bier, cartographer.

Index

Oregon Trail, 11–17, 19–26, 49–57, 60–65
orphans, x, 16, 47, 57
oxen, 14, 21, 30, 32, 60, 61

Pacific University, 16, 17
Peters, Charley, 65
picnic analogies, ix, 68
pies, 24, 72
Pikes Peak, 35, 38–40, 42
Plains Indians, 2
Platte River, 51, 53, 60, 77
political careers, 26, 40
Powder River, 82
Powers, Americus, 27, *28,* 29–31, 32
Powers, Celia, 27
Powers, Cephus, 27
Powers, Mary Rockwood, 27–34 , *28*
Powers, Sarah, 27, 34
pregnancies, 22, 25, 34, 59, 60, 79, 83
Pringle, Pherne, 11, 13, 14
Pringle, Virgil, 11, 13, 14, 15

quicksand, 3

rain, 11, 20, 21, 25, 43, 44, 50, 53, 56, 61
Raymond, Hillhouse, 71, 74
Raymond, Winthrop, 71, 74
Raymond Herndon, Sarah, 67– 75, *69*
Red Cloud, Chief, 80
Reed's Creek, 56
Republican River, 44, 45, 51
Ringo, Albert, 59
Ringo, Fanny Fern, 59–60
Ringo, Johnny, 59, 63, 65–66
Ringo, Martin, 59, 60, 61, 63
Ringo, Mary Enna, 59–60
Ringo, Mary Peters, 59– 66, *62*
Ringo Cushing, Matty Bell, 59–60, 65

river crossings
    animals resisting, 51
    dangers at, 3, 24, 44, 81
    toll bridges, 71
Rocky Mountains, 45–46
Royce, Josiah, 1, 2, 4
Royce, Josiah, Jr., 8
Royce, Mary, 1, 2, 4, 6
Royce, Sarah Eleanor Bayliss, 1–9

Sacramento Valley, 8, 56
sagebrush, 19, 24, 44
Salmon River, 24
Salt Lake City, Utah, 3, 64
San Leandro, California, 33
Santa Fe Trail, 35–40
schools, 16, 17, 75
Scotts Bluff, 53, 61
scurvy, 43
sheep trains, 32, 49–57
shortcuts, 14–15, 64, 80
Shoshones, 55
Sierra Nevada Mountains, 3, 7, 8, 33
Sioux, 78, 80
slaves, 41–42, 46, 47
Smoky Hill River, 44
Smoky Hill Trail, 41–46
snake bites, ix
Snake River, 24, 55
snow and snow storms, 7, 8, 15, 23, 40, 72
Snowdell, 39
Society of Colorado Pioneers, 48
South Pass, 64
South Platte River, 61, 71
Spanish Peaks, 40
starvation, 14
strawberries, 16, 32, 54
Sunday schools, 46
Sunday travel, 81
Sweetwater River, 23, 54, 64

About the Author

Mary Barmeyer O'Brien was born and raised in Missoula, Montana, and received a BA in sociology from Linfield College in McMinnville, Oregon. She is the author of eight previous books about women's history and pioneers on the overland trails, including *The Promise of the West: Young Pioneers on the Overland Trails, Jeannette Rankin: Bright Star in the Big Sky, Across Death Valley: The Pioneer Journey of Juliet Wells Brier, Outlasting the Trail: The Story of a Woman's Journey West*, and *May: The Hard-Rock Life of Pioneer May Arkwright Hutton* (all by TwoDot/Globe Pequot). Mary writes from her home in Polson, Montana, and enjoys hiking, camping, and reading. She and her husband, Dan, have three grown children and two grandchildren.

Acknowledgments

Heartfelt thanks to those who have contributed to the successful completion of this book, especially:

- Erin Turner and rest of the staff at Rowman & Littlefield, for their support and fine work;
- fellow writer Maggie Plummer, for her expert help and faithful encouragement;
- our son, Kevin D. O'Brien, for his drawing of a covered wagon, which is used on the title page and at the beginning of each chapter throughout this book;
- library director Marilyn Trosper at North Lake County Public Library in Polson, Montana, for her meticulous and conscientious research assistance;
- Melissa Guyles, for helping me visit those faraway research places;
- my family and friends for their good wishes; and
- the ten pioneer women who inspired this book by sharing their stories with us.

Many archivists, curators, and librarians along the way offered their expertise and assistance, including:

- Rachel Smith at the University of Wisconsin-Madison & Wisconsin State Historical Society Memorial Library;
- Laurie Klein of the Yale University Beinecke Library;
- Eleanor M. Gehres, manager of the Western History/ Genealogy Department of the Denver Public Library;
- Karyl Winn, curator of manuscripts, University of Washington Libraries, Seattle;

- Richard T. Read, university archivist/museum curator at Pacific University, Forest Grove, Oregon;
- the staff and volunteers at California's Huntington and Bancroft Libraries;
- Connie Geiger, archival technician at the Montana Historical Society; and
- the staff and volunteers at the End of the Oregon Trail Interpretive Center in Oregon City, Oregon; at the Replica of Old Fort Hall in Pocatello, Idaho; at the Clark County Historical Museum in Vancouver, Washington; and at the National Historic Trails Interpretive Center in Casper, Wyoming.

Many thanks also to the following archival sources for their kind assistance in providing materials:

- University of Washington Libraries for information on Amelia Stewart Knight.
- The Denver Public Library for information on Julia Anna Archibald.
- Pacific University Archives for information on Tabitha Moffatt Brown.
- The Yale University Beinecke Library for information on Martha Missouri Bishop Moore.
- The University of Wisconsin-Madison & Wisconsin State Historical Society Memorial Library for information on Martha Missouri Bishop Moore.

CPSIA information can be obtained
at www.ICGtesting.com
Printed in the USA
BVHW042255030321
601427BV00009B/18